FORTRAN 77 PDQ

/895

Brooks/Cole Brief Programming Guides

Program Design with Pseudocode, 3d Edition
T. W. Bailey & Kris Lundgaard

BASIC: An Introduction to Computer Programming, 3d Edition
Robert J. Bent & George C. Sethares

BASIC: An Introduction to Computer Programming with the Apple, 2nd Edition
Robert J. Bent & George C. Sethares

Microsoft BASIC: Programming the IBM PC, 2nd Edition
Robert J. Bent & George C. Sethares

Business BASIC, 3d Edition
Robert J. Bent & George C. Sethares

BASIC Programming with the IBM PC
Peter Mears

Basic Business BASIC Using the Apple, 2nd Edition
Peter Mears & Louis Raho

Absolutely BASIC Computing
Peter Mears

An Introduction to Personal Computing: BASIC Programming on the TRS-80
Robert R. Hare

Learning BASIC Programming: A Systematic Approach
Howard Dachslager, Masato Hayashi, & Richard Zucker

Beginning Structured COBOL, 2nd Edition
Keith Carver

Structured COBOL Programming and Data Processing Methods
Thomas R. McCalla

Problem Solving and Structured Programming with Pascal
Ali Behforooz & Martin O. Holoien

Pascal Programming
Irvine Forkner

Pascal for the Eighties
Samuel Grier

Problem Solving and Structured Programming with FORTRAN 77
Martin O. Holoien & Ali Behforooz

Introduction to ADA: A Top-Down Approach for Programmers
Phillip Caverly & Philip Goldstein

Introduction to DECSYSTEM-20 Assembly Programming
Stephen A. Longo

LOGO: Principles, Programming, and Projects
George Lukas & Joan Lukas

Second Edition

FORTRAN 77
PDQ[1]

Thomas A. Boyle
Purdue University

I don't know what the language of the year 2000 will look like, but I know it will be called Fortran. —Tony Hoare[2]

Brooks/Cole Publishing Company
Pacific Grove, California

Sponsoring Editor: Michael Sugarman
Editorial Supervisor: Joan Marsh
Production Service: InfoTech/Paul Quin
Manuscript Editor: Judy Kennedy
Interior Design: Paul Quin
Cover Design: Anderson & Associates/Barry Anderson
Typesetting: InfoTech
Printing: Malloy Lithographing

1. PDQ is Pretty Darn Quick, the way this book helps you learn Fortran.
2. C. A. R. (Tony) Hoare (1934–) is presently Director of the Computation Laboratory and Professor of Computing at Oxford University.

Brooks/Cole Publishing Company

A Division of Wadsworth, Inc.

10 9 8 7 6 5 4 3 2 1

Library of Congress Cataloging-in-Publication Data

Boyle, Thomas A.
       FORTRAN 77 PDQ

       Bibliography: p. 130
       Includes index.
       1. FORTRAN (Computer program language) I. Title.
II. Title: FORTRAN seventy-seven PDQ.
QA76.73.F25B69 1989   005.13'3   88-30476

ISBN 0-534-09936-X

Preface

The primary goal in the preparation of **Fortran 77 PDQ** has been to provide adequate textual material to support the learning efforts of would-be programmers with little previous computer-related experience. The intended adequacy is for the broad range of learners who, in great majority, will not pursue programming as their principal work. Rather, they will make occasional use of a computer as a tool, preparing programs that, after being checked out, will usually be run only a few times. As used here, the word *adequate* first means complete with respect to the needs of a typical learner for text material. The word further means that the included information is accessible to a typical learner within the limits of time that will reasonably be devoted to the related learning.

A second goal has been the identification of three levels of skill in Fortran programming, and the specification of these levels in operational terms. In general, the first skill level includes these abilities:

- to enter a program and retrieve output
- to program computations in real and integer modes
- to use elementary loops, the logical IF, and the block IF
- to use selected library functions
- to program input and output with free-format.

Students who have progressed to the second level will readily demonstrate the use of:

- character data
- singly-subscripted variables
- nesting of loops and blocks
- formatted input and output.

Learners in the third skill level will demonstrate confident use of:

- multiple subscripts
- user subprograms
- Fortran's three remaining data types
- programmed file management.

A rationale for program planning and a brief introduction to top-down design is presented in the fourth chapter, and a quick guide to many of Fortran's most used forms is included for ready reference. Exercises throughout the text allow students to practice skills as they are introduced.

A word is in order regarding the ordering of topics. First, although no proscription is maintained against the GO TO, its introdution is no longer featured in the first programming of loops. The implied suggestion for those with simple needs is to use only counter-controlled loops. This may necessitate a pilot run or two to determine the number of iterations to obtain the desired result, or programming some iterations that are not needed. Occasional programmers seeking condition control of loops encounter first the WHILE, then the GO TO. The intent here is that if WHILE is available, GO TO will be needed only infrequently. If WHILE is not now available, it will probably be soon; until then, use GO TO sparingly and with due care.

Single subscripts are introduced early because they are so inherently powerful. Unfortunately, the concurrent mathematics studied by most students does not get to arrays until some time after they are encountered in the pursuit of programming, making the learning of subscripts difficult for many. Nonetheless, ability with single subscripts is advocated for practically all who attempt programming; an increase in complexity of one order yields an increase of at least two orders in programming power. Further, the greater the extent of experience with single subscripts, the greater the probability of success with double subscripts. For some occasional programmers, double subscripts themselves may not be worthwhile; the power-to-complexity ratio is not nearly so favorable for learning double subscripts as it is for learning single subscripts.

Fortran 77 PDQ was developed to meet the textual needs of students concurrently pursuing course work in mathematics and physics, and often in chemistry as well. Although reliable design criteria are difficult to come by, for the purposes of this book, we assume that the total time commitment by the average student learning Fortran can be no more than half the time spent by the same student in the concurrent pursuit of physics. This suggests a maximum of 100 hours for the average student in a typical semester. A further time breakdown among class participation, working at a terminal, and reading the text leads to an estimate of from 8 to 12 hours as the optimum time for a student to spend with a Fortran text in hand.

Currently (1988), the great majority of the intended group of students acknowledges some computer-related experience. Most of the experience reported is programming in Basic with some Pascal programming and a measure of computer literacy. The continuing popularity of Basic and the rising popularity of Pascal in secondary schools indicate Fortran will be the second computer language for many, if not most, students. Trends in other quarters suggest Fortran has passed its prime and will soon be replaced, if indeed individual programming itself is not replaced. Another view of the real world holds that, like the railroad and the piston engine, Fortran has become a part of us and will continue to serve us for a long time.

My thanks to the students and teachers who have used this book and whose comments have helped make this second edition more useful, especially those colleagues who reviewed the manuscript: Robert Barnes, Lehigh University; Stephen Beck, Bloomsburg University; Kenneth Kopecky, Drake University; Eric Pas, Duke University; and Robert Stanton, St. John's University.

Thomas A. Boyle

Contents

Chapter 1

A First Level of Programming Skill

1.1   Fortran 2
1.2   Operating Systems 3
1.3   Inevitable Preliminaries 3
1.4   Terminals 3
1.5   Files 5
1.6   Editing 6
1.7   Computing Something 6
1.8   Ordering of Operations 9
1.9   Getting Results Out 10
1.10   Finishing the Program 11
1.11   Exercises 1-1 13
1.12   Type Considerations I 15
1.13   Integers 16
1.14   Integer Variables 17
1.15   Integer Arithmetic 17
1.16   Exponentiation with Integers 18
1.17   Looping Operations I 18
1.18   Fortran's DO 18
1.19   Labeling with Free-Format 21
1.20   Exercises 1-2 22
1.21   Conditional Execution 25
1.22   Relational Operators 26
1.23   Reading with Free-Format 27
1.24   Block IF 30
1.25   IF-THEN-ELSE 32
1.26   Library Functions 33
1.27   Program Troubles 36
1.28   Exercises 1-3 39
1.29   Summary for Level One 42

Chapter 2

Intermediate Programming Skills

2.1   Type Considerations II 44
2.2   Type Declaration 44
2.3   Type Conversion 45
2.4   Integer Functions 45

2.5	CHARACTER	46
2.6	Substrings	47
2.7	Character Functions	48
2.8	Exercises 2-1	49
2.9	Subscripted Variables I	50
2.10	Looping Operations II	55
2.11	Nested DO Loops	55
2.12	Implied DO Loops	57
2.13	Sorting Example	58
2.14	Exercises 2-2	62
2.15	WHILE Loops	63
2.16	Fortran's GO TO	64
2.17	Formatted Output	65
2.18	Exponential Form and E FORMAT	68
2.19	Labeling Formatted Output	70
2.20	Exercises 2-3	71
2.21	INTEGER FORMAT	73
2.22	Alphanumeric FORMAT	73
2.23	Reading with FORMAT Control	73
2.24	DATA	77
2.25	Exercises 2-4	78
2.26	Summary for Level Two	81

Chapter 3

Toward Powerful Programming

3.1	Subscripted Variables II, Double Subscripts	83
3.2	Graphic Output with Double Subscripts	87
3.3	Exercises for Double Subscripts	89
3.4	User Subprograms	90
3.5	User Subprograms I, Statement Functions	91
3.6	User Subprograms II, Function Subprograms	92
3.7	User Subprograms III, Subroutines	95
3.8	Subprogram Exercises	96
3.9	Arrays as Subprogram Arguments	97
3.10	Subprograms with Adjustable Arrays	98
3.11	INTRINSIC and EXTERNAL	100
3.12	COMMON	101
3.13	Subroutine Example	102
3.14	Labeled COMMON	103
3.15	LOGICAL	104
3.16	Multiple-Consideration Decisions	105
3.17	Multiple-Alternative Decisions	106
3.18	Multiple Subscripts	107
3.19	DODUBLE PRECISION	108
3.20	COMPLEX	110

3.21 Programmed File Management 111
3.22 Direct Access Files 113
3.23 Sequential Access Files 116
3.24 File Management Exercises 118
3.25 Implicit Type Declaration 118
3.26 PARAMETER 119
3.27 Looping Operations III 119
3.28 Computed GO TO 120
3.29 EQUIVALENCE 121
3.30 Summary for Level Three 122

Chapter 4
Delayed Preliminaries

4.1 Program Planning 124
4.2 Flowcharts 125
4.3 Pseudocode 126
4.4 Top-Down Program Design 127
4.5 Program Documentation 130
4.6 Summary 130

References 131

Quick Guide to Frequently-Used Fortran Forms 132

Index 137

Chapter 1

A First Level of Programming Skill

You have to start from somewhere. Why not start from where you are? —W. Robert Sands, Jr.[1]

This introduction to computer programming is intended for beginners. Its purpose is to help beginners develop adequate skill in using Fortran to prepare instructions for a computer. Presumably, each person undertaking such activity has a need that some measure of programming ability will help satisfy. At the outset, all should recognize a tradeoff inherent in the pursuit of programming skill. If it suits their purpose, some may proceed only to the mastery of a few, simple program elements. These may be adequate for the purposes at hand. But such programmers must be content with relatively long programs made up of many simple elements. Other persons may want to master more powerful, and necessarily more complicated, program elements. For a given task, their programs will consist of fewer elements and, at least in principle, should require less time to prepare. For one destined to be an occasional programmer, the depth to which related skills are to be pursued is an individual matter. Each must decide for himself or herself how much is enough.

Regardless of the level of programming skill to which one aspires, we must attend to several matters at the beginning. These become primary objectives for all who seek to enlist a computer's help. First, the potential programmer must become familiar with the physical equipment available and with applicable protocol. Next, the person must establish communication with the computer. Only after achieving a measure of

---

1. W. Robert Sands, Jr. (1906–1979) graduated from the U. S. Naval Academy in 1926 and pursued graduate study at Purdue University. In 1964 he was a senior power consultant in the Engineering Department of E. I. duPont de Nemours & Co.

success with these two objectives can one come to grips with the business of preparing a first program. To a certain degree the preparation of the first computer program is like the solo flight of an airplane pilot. In each event recently learned skills are put to the test. If the desired learning has been done by the pilot, then the takeoff, climb, left and right turns, and finally the landing proceed in the way planned. If the necessary skills are in place within the fledgling programmer, the preparation and entry of the program is duly followed by the retrieval of some output. However, a substantial difference exists between the typical performance within the two groups. Fortunately, the overwhelming majority of solo pilots achieve success with their initial efforts. In some contrast the majority, or at least a very substantial minority, of fledgling programmers are less than successful with their initial efforts. In the jargon of the trade we say their programs crash. Fortunately program crashes seldom result in bodily injury.

You do not have to take flying lessons to realize that loop-the-loops and Immelmann turns are not generally featured in the instruction first given to pilots. The beginning pilot is restrained to master a minimum adequate set of skills, enough to get from here to there and back and land without mishap. Similarly, most beginning programmers will find their way easier if at first their attention is restricted to a minimum set of programming skills. These five skills, then, become the objectives for all who seek a first level of programming ability:

1. Demonstrate success in preparing and running a straight-through program, one in which the result obtained in one program step is used in a subsequent step, and so on.
2. Distinguish between Fortran's two principal data types and demonstrate advantageous use of each type.
3. Apply looping in program situations that otherwise would require repeated sections of similar instructions.
4. Demonstrate conditional execution of single program steps and of groups of program steps.
5. Identify and use several of the library functions that are available to all Fortran programmers.

Having thus identified the initial objectives for all who would program, let's turn to the business of attaining the first level of proficiency.

1.1 Fortran

Computer pioneers developed Fortran to provide escape from the tedium of preparing instructions in the native language, that is, **machine language**, of available computers. Fortran is at once a set of rules humans must follow to prepare computer instructions and the capacity for translating these human-generated instructions into machine language. We refer to the language with which humans work when preparing instructions as **Fortran**. The capacity for translating the instructions resides in computer programs called **Fortran compilers**. The machine languages and the compilers for two computers may be substantially different, but a proper Fortran program will yield the same result when compiled and run on either machine. In each case the actual processing of data is done in the machine's own language. It would make little difference to the computer whether the machine-language instructions were produced from a Fortran program by a compiler, or prepared by a dedicated human programming directly in machine language. But for most humans, programming in Fortran is much more practical than working with any computer's machine language.

1.2 Operating Systems

The procedures followed in processing a Fortran program are more involved than those for running programs in some other languages. Furthermore, most computer installations capable of processing Fortran also serve programmers who use other languages. Such circumstances necessitate some control of the flow of jobs to the computer, making sure that the many services needed by each job are available at the proper time. Conceivably this could be done by a nimble human, for instance making sure that the Fortran compiler was ready, then an instant later dispatching the machine-language instructions for execution. In practice these functions are almost always performed by another program, the **operating system**. Typically the operating system senses the requirements of an oncoming job by first interpreting the control statements which precede the actual program. These control statements include the programmer's identification and password. The procedures followed when providing user identification and requesting system capabilities are different for each system.

1.3 Inevitable Preliminaries

Before implementing any Fortran program some preliminaries must be satisfied. Although the focus in most of the following sections is on the preparation of the program itself, a brief survey of these preliminaries may provide a beneficial starting point. The preliminaries here refer to the need to establish communication with the computer. This need directs attention to the topics of **terminals, files**, and **editing**.

1.4 Terminals

Contemporary communication between humans and computers is dominated by devices called **terminals**. These transform the depressing of a typewriter-like, character key into a unique electric signal ready to be fed to a computer. Concurrent with the generation of each signal, the corresponding character appears, either on a television-like screen or typed on paper. The appearance of the character enables the human to check each character group, or string, as it is to be entered. The completion of each character group, which is to make up an instruction or a row of data, is confirmed by depressing a **return**, or **new-line**, key. The terminal action here is similar to that of a mechanical typewriter when the carriage is returned to prepare for typing a new line. (We know that nobody makes mechanical typewriters anymore, so you will just have to use your imagination or watch the part of an electric machine that does the printing.) The signal generated by terminal processing of one or more characters can be sent directly to a computer, or the resulting information can be accumulated for later transfer.

Although terminals are undergoing continuing development and may differ in some specific details, the following features are practically universal:

1. **The standard typewriter-like keyboard.** This is readily identified by the key sequence "QWERTY" in a row near the keyboard's upper left-hand side. The whole set of keys enables entry of letters, numerals, punctuation, and special-purpose characters.

2. **A RETURN or NEW-LINE key.** This key **must be depressed after practically all keyboard entries**. Beginners waste lots of time waiting for something to happen, while their terminals are waiting for them to signal RETURN or NEW LINE.

3. **A SHIFT key.** This key enables a single character key to signal either a lowercase or uppercase letter, or alternatively a numeral or punctuation character or a special symbol. The SHIFT key is held down while depressing a letter or other character key. For example, an action designated as SHIFT-A would yield a capital A. This operation is the same as that of a standard typewriter.

4. **A CONTROL, or CTRL, key.** This key enables yet a different signal to be generated by a familiar letter key. The action is similar to that with the SHIFT key, but the results are distinctly different. For example, holding down the CONTROL key and depressing the letter D (CTRL-D) yields something quite remote from an uppercase letter dee! Plan on learning several character combinations that get started by holding down the CTRL key.

5. **One or more ESCAPE, BREAK, or RESET keys.** These keys enable recovery from minor foul-ups, or relief from having to view a lengthy sequence of already-familiar instructions for the umpteenth time. The labeling and key functions are not standardized, so counsel from someone familiar with the terminal system you are to use is probably in order. Or perhaps you favor fearless experimentation.

In addition to the aforementioned standard and special-purpose keys, beginning programmers can frequently find key combinations that will lock up the keyboard. These are not usually well advertised, but many beginners find them with little effort. If you manage to discover a combination that apparently disables your terminal, don't become alarmed. There is little chance that a human, using fingers, will do serious damage either to or via a terminal. Remember, too, that even the best of machines and operating systems occasionally go awry. If terminal lock-up or malfunction should befall you, don't panic. Try turning the terminal off, waiting a moment or two and then turning it back on. At all times rest assured your terminal is doing its best to serve you.

Chances are you will develop true affection for your terminal, although it may not be love at first sight.

1.5 Files

Program instructions, or data to be processed at a terminal are accumulated in **files**. Files are chunks of information. They can be very small, or very large, or any size in between. A file could contain only one letter or numeral; another could hold all the information in the phone book for a large city. The files of present interest will be small to medium in size. They will hold the instructions making up Fortran programs. They will also hold instructions to the operating system that is to run the programs. Other files considered later will hold data to be read in and processed by the Fortran programs. Before you can make much progress in programming, some skill in file manipulation is a practical necessity. The details of file creation and editing are certainly not the same for all systems. In most instances this means a period devoted to learning the file-handling capabilities (and idiosyncrasies) of the system that is to process your program. Most beginners find their file-manipulating skills and their programming skills develop in tandem.

Notwithstanding the differences in file management encountered on different systems, several characteristics are sufficiently common to serve as starting points. The first of these is that all files must have names. Most systems provide some latitude in establishing file names, so we can usually adopt names that contain clues regarding the file contents, just as you would likely do when labeling the tabs of paper folders to be stored in a filing cabinet. You may find that a file can be built up or created without designating the file name. But a name is required if the information is to be saved. The same name will be essential when the information is to be retrieved.

Most beginners find that they quickly accumulate a number of files, thus creating a need for a way to keep track of their handiwork. The desired capacity is usually available in the form of a **catalog** or **directory**. Either of these lists the names of all files present in a particular file space, for example, in the part of a storage disk assigned to an individual user. Each entry in a catalog or directory represents a file. This arrangement helps absent-minded participants who forget file names. The listing of the catalog or directory enables recall of the file names and, if suitable names have been chosen, gives at least an inkling as to the file contents.

Next, with regard to describing files, the reference frame provided by **rows**, or **lines**, and **columns** seems invaluable. When appearing on a terminal screen or as printed on paper, the characters in a file are arranged in rows. These may contain as few as 20 characters, as they appear on some terminal screens, or as many as 130 in the file listings produced by line printers or printing terminals. Specific positions along a row, counting from left to right, are designated by columns. Files are created one row at a time, just as you would produce a typewritten letter. Characters are entered or columns are skipped along each row beginning with column one. In files that are to become Fortran programs, most of the characters are put in the column range beginning with column seven and none extends farther than column 72.

1.6 Editing

If one were content with very simple programs, then the need to make changes in a program file might not be a serious matter. If we discovered an error, we could abandon the file and create a new, error-free file. This procedure would certainly lack appeal for any but very short files and short programs. Practical circumstances require the ability to correct and change files. This capability is generally available in a system program, the **editor**. Usually the editor is involved in the creation of files, although its service may not be noticed. But the editor is essential when an error is detected in any substantial file. We then can invoke the editor to make the necessary changes. Other circumstances prompt the use of the editor's ability to add or delete lines and, for example, to copy or rename entire files. You will quickly learn to appreciate the service provided by your system's editor.

Having attended to some preliminaries, our consideration can shift to the preparation of a simple program. This will introduce the minimal set of Fortran elements with which a beginner can fashion a successful program. Next, we urge all beginners to try preparing programs of their own. Thereafter, as additional elements are introduced, they are illustrated with example programs. A manageable number of new features will be presented in each example. Examples are accompanied by programming exercises in which the new elements are to be used. Each person attending to the sequence of exercises will build on programs that he or she has prepared and run. Truly, there is no substitute for the experience of preparing, and then repairing, your own programs as they take on increasing levels of complexity. Students attempting to bypass the preparation of their own simple programs succeed principally in making their learning difficult.

1.7 Computing Something

Consider the way in which humans communicate the simplest of operations a computer might be called upon to do. "Add 62.0 to 34.0," we might say if our native language were English. Alternatively, we could convey the same message using arithmetic symbols, for example:

```
34.0
62.0                          or                34.0 + 62.0
────
```

Along about the fifth grade most children have grasped the intent represented in either of these groups of symbols. With a little encouragement they will enter the sum below the line in the configuration on the left, and to the right in the other configuration, separating the sum from the addend by the equals symbol. Most of us have been performing this sort of operation for some time. Along the way we have adopted certain conventions. For example, we enter the sum below the line in the configuration on the left. The configuration on the right is a bit less convention-bound. An equals sign could be placed either to the right of the 62.0 or to the left of the 34.0. Most people would understand the signal either way and would put the sum in the intended location. We could say that the equals symbol separates the other symbols, those representing the intended operation, from the location in which the result of the operation is to be put. When communicating with other humans, the preferred location for the result is indicated by the location of the equals symbol.

When communicating in Fortran, the equals symbol **always** appears to the left of the characters representing the desired operation. Fortran-speaking computers insist on this. If an unwary programmer attempts to perform part of an algebraic operation on the left side of the equals sign, then disaster, in the form of a crashed program, is assured. Perhaps you are wondering what does belong to the left of the equals sign. The character or characters there are interpreted as the **name** by which the result of the operation will be identified. This name will be necessary if the result is to be used in a subsequent operation in the program. It will also be essential if we ask the computer to tell us the result it obtained.

Taken together, the name, the equals symbol, and all the characters and symbols representing the operation make up a Fortran **instruction** or **statement**. Such statements are the principal elements in Fortran programs. It is through a sequence of statements that we obtain the desired result. The general form of such a Fortran statement can be represented as follows:

```
NAME  =  OPERATION
```

Here the word *"OPERATION"* represents any of the countless operations that a computer could be called upon to do. Some Fortraners favor the word **"expression"** (that is, the group of symbols representing the operation) instead of the word "operation." Either way, try to think of each step of the desired action as being directed by the symbols appearing on the right side of an equals sign. In Fortran statements the equals sign separates the operation, or expression if you prefer, from what happens to the result of the operation after it is completed.

When considering each Fortran statement, look first at the operation part, the part on the right side of the equals sign. For example, the expression:

```
=  34.0  +  62.0
```

specifies an operation in which 34.0 is added to 62.0. As each operation is completed, the result becomes the new value to be identified by the name appearing on the left side of the equals symbol. We say the result of the operation is attached to, or **assigned** to, the designated name. All this is done by our old friend, the equals sign; some insist on calling it by a new name, the **assignment operator**. After a value has been assigned to a name, the name may appear in subsequent operations. In such use the value assigned to the name will be used wherever the name appears.

One of the simplest Fortran statements involves only the assignment of a value to the name. As an example, consider the following:[2]

```
7
ABB  =  3.4
```

---

2. The 7 here appears above the character represented as appearing in column 7, for example, in a row of information prepared on a terminal or on a punched card. In general, Fortran statements begin in column 7 and extend no farther than column 72.

Here the value 3.4 is assigned to the name ABB. It makes no difference what value ABB may have had before; the previously held value is forgotten when a new value is assigned to a name. An assigned value can be replaced by a subsequent assignment. The value associated with ABB can be changed by assigning it a new value. For instance, the statement:

```
7
ABB  =  729.8
```

will assign the new value of 729.8 to ABB. The name ABB can have only one value at a time, so each new assignment replaces the old one.

Inasmuch as ABB can be assigned different values, it is evidently different from the number 3.4. The latter has one value for all time; the 3.4 is quite properly considered to be a **constant**. In contrast, the name ABB can take on practically any value, and its value can be changed as many times as we please. The name ABB, as well as a great many similar groups of characters, is referred to as a **variable**. Since numerals can be included with letters in variable names, you can probably think of a great many names for variables. The suitability of these names will be assured if the following points are observed:

1. Start variable names with a letter of the alphabet. For present purposes use letters from A to H or from O to Z. Save the letters from I to N for later use.

2. Use only letters and numerals; do not use punctuation, blanks, or special characters.

3. Use no more than six characters in a variable name.

The data processing operations considered thus far prompt consideration of a simple arithmetic operation expressed as a Fortran statement. Here the expression "add 62.0 to 34.0" must be extended to include the name by which the result will be identified. For instance, "add 62.0 to 34.0 and call the result CAB" presents the essential characteristics of the desired operation and specifies the name to be used if we want to pursue the matter further. In Fortran this would appear as:

```
7
CAB  =  62.0  +  34.0
```

or, if we preferred to have names for everything:

```
7
C = 62.0
B = 34.0
ABC = C + B
```

In the first instance, the single operation simply adds the two constants, as you would do with an adding machine. The result of the operation, the sum, is then assigned to the variable named CAB. In the second instance, designated values are first assigned to variables C and B. The final statement directs addition of the values held by these variables and then the result being assigned to ABC. Observe that the three statements are executed in their top-to-bottom order. And try to appreciate the difficulty in executing the last statement if values had not been previously assigned to C and B. Be forewarned that such use of a variable, without previously assigning it a value, will prompt many Fortran compilers to grumble something about an undefined variable.

1.8 Ordering of Operations

The operations represented in most Fortran statements are more involved than those introduced so far. For example, the statement:

```
.
B44 = (A9 - C)/A6
.
```

directs an operation which includes subtraction and division. The dots, here shown before and after the statement, are to indicate that it is one of a sequence, presumably making up a program. This statement directs the difference between the current values of variables A9 and C to be divided by the current value of variable A6. Rest assured, the computer will treat A9 and A6 as different variables, even though both names begin with the letter A. If the statement is to be successfully executed, then values for variables A9, C, and A6 must have been established in preceding statements which are not shown. The values could have been established by simple assignment of a constant's value, or by assignment of the result from operations, or from data read in from an external source. The example statement will result in assignment of some value to variable B44, so it can appear in the operation part of subsequent statements.

Observe the use of parentheses, or **parens,** in the example; they direct the subtraction to be done before the division. The order of arithmetic operations would be different if the parens were not present; the division would be done first, then the resulting quotient subtracted from the value of A9. When in any doubt about the ordering of arithmetic operations, a programmer should use parentheses to make the intended order of operations inescapable. The only caution here is to be sure that the number of close, or right, parens equals the number of open, or left, parens. Fortran compilers are sticklers for details like that.

Most readers will note similarities between the representation of ordinary mathematics and the grouping of symbols making up the operation parts of Fortran statements. Not until one advances to multiplication is any difference evident. Here there are two differences. First, the asterisk is the Fortran symbol used for multiplication. For example:

```
.
BBB = 3.0 * B
.
```

results in the present value of variable B being multiplied by the constant 3.0 (for now, remember to include decimal points with the constants) and the product being named BBB. The asterisk was adopted as the multiplication symbol in Fortran to preclude confusing those of us who tried to use the letter X as both the multiplication symbol and a variable name. So, remember to use the asterisk for multiplying in Fortran, even if you can't say "asterisk." Remember too, you must **always** use it whenever multiplication is desired. Combinations of symbols such as 3.0B, which are clear to you and me, cause a Fortran-speaking computer all kinds of distress. The compiler keeps trying to interpret this as a name, and it knows that names can't start with numerals; it never suspects that multiplication was intended because no asterisk appears. If you use such a combination of symbols, the poor computer will mumble some apology about not being able to recognize the name.

So far you have met all but one of the Fortran representations for arithmetic operations. The missing link is **exponentiation,** and this is directed by a pair of asterisks. For example:

```
AAA = A ** 2.8
```

results in the current value of variable A being raised to the 2.8 power and then stored as the new value of variable AAA. If you need to program exponentiation to whole-number powers, use repeated multiplication. Use Z*Z*Z instead of Z**3.0 because computers usually do multiplications faster than exponentiations.

The normal order in which Fortran processes arithmetic operations is as follows:

1. Exponentiations are done first (from right to left).

2. Multiplications and divisions are done next (proceeding from left to right).

3. Additions and subtractions are done last (again from left to right).

This normal order can be modified by using parens. When in doubt about the ordering of arithmetic operations, use parens to assure the order you intend. And, if you use 12 open parens in the representation of an operation, take care to include a dozen close parens.

The preceding paragraphs are intended to introduce only enough Fortran elements for performing the simplest of computational jobs. Next, consider the elements of Fortran that persuade the computer to let us know the results of its efforts.

1.9 Getting Results Out

In some contrast to earlier versions of Fortran, contemporary models simplify the business of obtaining output. Earlier Fortrans would never reveal the results of their efforts unless they had been told specifically where to put those results (for example, in a particular group, or field, of ten columns in a row, with the decimal point located just so). Lots of would-be programmers became so distraught with the related details (that is, formatting the output) that they gave up Fortran completely. Fortunately some stalwarts resolved to better the lot of the programmers who would follow. A noteworthy result of their efforts is available in the **free-format** or **list-directed output** capability which most beginners use, but will probably never appreciate. This all works with the PRINT* instruction. If a PRINT* instruction were added to a previous sequence of three statements, the result would be:

```
C = 62.0
B = 34.0
ABC = C + B
PRINT*, C, B, ABC
```
.

Evidently the PRINT* instruction is to cause the current values of variables C, B, and ABC to be printed, either at the terminal or by a line printer. In the terms of the trade, we speak of the C, B, ABC part as a list of variables, and the PRINT* is said to yield list-directed output. Notice that the list is separated from the PRINT* instruction by a comma, that the variables in the list are separated by commas, and that **no comma** follows the last variable in the list. If a comma were to follow the last variable, the poor compiler would waste a lot of time looking for another variable.

The numerical output from our example PRINT* would appear more or less as follows:

```
62.00000000000    34.00000000000    96.00000000000
```

The "more or less" is included here because the configuration, or formatting of the output (that is, the number of digits and the width of the space, or **field**, to accommodate each value and the number of blank spaces between fields) may be different for different implementations of Fortran. The example output includes 13 numerals plus a decimal point for each value. Inasmuch as space must be provided for a negative sign, we can confirm the width of the field accommodating each value to be at least 15 columns. The width of field provided by free-format may vary a bit, depending on the particular Fortran. Very large or very small values may appear in atypical fields. Some may appear in exponential form; in this form four characters at the right of the field indicate the powers of ten to be incorporated into the value shown. For example, in 3.456E+03, the E+03 indicates the value 3.456 is to be multiplied by 10.0*10.0*10.0. In any case, free-format will put the decimal point in a good spot for the size of the number being printed.

Some Fortran implementations do not recognize the PRINT* instruction, so alternative procedures are in order. If yours is one of the Fortrans that responds in this way, try the following in place of the PRINT*:

```
WRITE(*,*) C, B, ABC
```

Still other versions of Fortran expect a number in place of the first asterisk within the parens. The number identifies one of the available output devices, say the line printer or the terminal screen. In the form shown here, the first asterisk usually refers to the primary output device, in most instances the terminal screen.

1.10 Finishing the Program

The preceding sections present practically all the Fortran needed in a simple computer program. The remaining element is one to advise the compiler that it has worked its way through the program and has come to the end. Fittingly enough the statement that does this vital job is the **END** statement and it must appear last in every Fortran program. With END appended, our first example program appears as follows:

```
C = 62.0
B = 34.0
ABC = C + B
PRINT*, C, B, ABC
END
```

When contemplating any program, even one as simple as this example, make sure all statements begin in a position corresponding to column 7, or at least not before column 7. Remember, too, that statements cannot extend beyond column 72. If you form a statement that is too long to fit within these limits, break the operation (everything on the right side of the equals sign) into parts. Assign the result of the first part of the operation to some variable, then use that variable in a statement that includes the second part of the operation, and so on. In general, try to program with more short statements, rather than with a few long ones. Errors in long statements can be difficult to locate and fix. When you use short statements, it is easier to check the results obtained at each step along the way.

Next, be sure to include program statements to produce output. The convenience of the PRINT* instruction makes this part of your program easy. Many beginners tend to be miserly in programming for output. For instance, in the example at hand they would print only the value of variable ABC. But it is no more costly nor time consuming to provide for the output of the values of variables C and B, too. And always remember, the only way to be **sure** of the value that has been established for a variable at a particular point in your program is to have the value printed out. So be liberal in programming for output, especially in your early efforts and whenever you have trouble with a program. When in doubt about a program, insert PRINT* instruction after every other statement. Get in the habit of making the computer tell everything about what it is doing. You will be glad you did.

Having confirmed these conditions and made sure the END statement is there, the program is ready to be submitted for processing. Unless you are using your very own computer, you will have to make provisions for the program to be accepted by the system you are using. At this point we must face the fact that every system is different from every other system. No matter where your program is to be run, you must attend to the details regarding its control in the stream of programs to be processed. The system regards each separate program as a job to be done, and the management of all these jobs is referred to as job control. In general, a few job control instructions will precede your program into the computer. One will carry a number or character set which enables identification of the output from your program. Another will hold information about who you are and tell which account to charge for the computer time and paper consumed. Other instructions may specify the maximum amount of time to devote to your job. Do not become unduly concerned with the details of job control during your early attempts at communicating with a computer. Get help from someone familiar with job control on the computer system you are using and try one or two of the exercises.

1.11 Exercises 1-1

Most participants will find the pursuit of early exercises necessitates both practice with an editor as well as practice with the elements of Fortran encountered thus far. Solutions for the present exercise set are intended to be relatively long, one pass (no looping) programs that provide substantial opportunity for developing editor skills and opportunity for discovering the ways and the wiles of Fortran, or preferably both. The exercises are usually amenable to checking with hand computation or through reference to generally available mathematics tables. Respondents approaching adequacy in the development of their editor skills will find these exercises easy to do in a short time, for example, by using their editor's line-copying facility to repeat sections of program instructions. Others must either take the time to develop the editor skills or resign themselves to the task of entering lots of repetitive lines in their programs. For your efforts with this exercise set please restrict all variables to those beginning with letters in the A–H range and include decimal points with all program constants.

1. Extend the example program to include all five arithmetic operations. Confirm the ordering of multiplication and division to go from left to right, and that the ordering of exponentiation goes from right to left. Demonstrate the use of parens to alter the default ordering of multiplication, division and exponentiation.

2. Run a program that will establish the value of

    $$X^5 - 3X^4 + 5X^3 - 7X^2 + 12X - 10$$

    for $X = 2.0, 4.0, \ldots 20.0$.

3. Prepare a program that will produce a brief multiplication table. Have the multiplicands appear in the left hand column and show the multipliers in a row across the top. Free-format, or list-directed, output limits the number of output columns so you will either restrict your multipliers to the range 1–5, or use even numbers; in either case, extend your range of multiplicands at least to 10.0. Practice with different combinations of multipliers and multiplicands until you can program the production of an example table within say, ten or fifteen minutes.

4. The following groups of letters, numerals, and punctuation marks have features that make them unsuitable for use either as variables or as constants in a Fortran program.

ROGER,T	2,3	X-5
456780.948	-E03	3.4.5
987,123.0456	TOM.BOY	3.14X10-2
A=B=C	68A79.3	1,23E-04
INEQUALITY	+E-15	3.4,5.1

    Consider each group in turn and decide whether it was intended for use as a constant or a variable, then see if you can identify the flaw that makes the group unsuitable for the intended use. Be sensitive to the distinction between the numeral zero and the letter that follows N in our alphabet. If you have trouble finding the flaw, try using the character group in a very short Fortran program.

5. The factorial of a number is the continued product of all whole numbers up to and including the number. For example 3 factorial (3!) is the product of 1 times 2 times 3. Prepare a program to produce the sequence of factorials up to 20!. Note possible changes in the form of the output as the values become larger.

6. Program the production of successive rows of output in which the first entry represents a diameter, the second the circumference of a circle with the given diameter, the third the area of the circle, then the surface area of a sphere with the given diameter and finally the volume of the sphere.

7. Lucky Pierre has a job for which he receives a gross pay of $800.00 per month. Federal income tax of 14 percent is withheld first, then the state gets 6 percent of what Pierre has left after the federal tax is withheld. The local tax is 3 percent of the remainder after federal and state taxes, but $150.00 per month is exempt from the local tax. If $40.00 is withheld to cover Pierre's health and accident insurance, and if he agrees to contribute 4 percent of his "after tax" pay to the united fund, then determine Pierre's take home pay. After all the computations are finished have your program print out all amounts arranged in a column; don't worry about putting labels on each amount just yet, attaching labels to program output will be treated in a soon-to-come section.

8. Recently Fudd's market has been having difficulty retaining competent delivery boys and girls; they work for a week or so, then quit. A new pay scale has been devised and your task is to produce a listing of each day's wages for a month together with the number of the day and the cumulative wages for the month. Pay starts at the modest rate of $0.25 per day, but increases $0.25 each of the first ten days. During the next ten days the wages increase 10 percent each day, and from then until the 31st the increase is 12 percent each day. Why not use variable names that suggest their purpose in the program, for example, DAY, ADAY, and ATOT or something equally appropriate?

9. The future worth of $100.00 invested with compound interest accruing at four percent can be represented as DLRS = 100.0*(1.0+0.04)**AYRS, where DLRS is the future worth after the investment accumulates interest for a period of AYRS years. Program the preparation of a table showing the future worth of $100.00 invested at several rates of interest that include the rates currently typical for both borrowers and lenders; show values for each year up to 20.

10. Check the sequence $4.0 - 4.0/3.0 + 4.0/5.0 - 4.0/7.0 + 4.0/9.0 \ldots$ and confirm the report that it provides an estimate of *pi*. Run a program that includes at least 20 terms to obtain your approximation. To do this you will need to work with groups of terms to avoid having code extend beyond column 72. Sum all the terms that fit on a program line and assign the sum to a variable; do this for two or three groups of terms, then sum the two or three variables. Using 3.14159 as the reference value, determine the amount of error in your estimate and the percent error.

11. An expedition has recently returned from studying conditions on the mysterious planet Carto, where the fundamental units of mass, distance and time are respectively the MOGG, the DWAZA, and the TAMPA. As you would expect, the most elementary force unit, the FUBAR, will, when acting on a mass of one MOGG, yield an acceleration of one DWAZA per TAMPA squared. Gravitational acceleration is not very uniform on Carto, varying from 3.6 D per T squared at the equator to 5.4 at the poles. Your task is to run a program that will produce a table of distances that a mass will fall from rest when under the influence of Cartovian gravity for times up to 20 TAMPAs. Cover the noted range of gravity in increments that take full advantage of the number of columns you get when using free–format output control.

1.12 Type Considerations I

By limiting variable names to those beginning with letters in the A–H, or O–Z range, and by using only constants with decimal points, a programmer is restricted to one type of Fortran element or **data type**. The standard name for this type is **real**. Accordingly we say the variables considered thus far are **real variables**, and all those constants with the decimal points included are **real constants**. As you probably suspect by now, there are other types of Fortran elements. Here the word "type" refers to the nature of the data or information that can be represented by a constant or accommodated by a variable. Each data type, or **mode**, has advantages for some purposes, but each is subject to disadvantages when used for other purposes.

The second Fortran type to be considered is **integer**. This is the type of data derived from counting whole things, say the number of persons in a theater or the number of automobiles stopped by a traffic signal. Fortran's integer mode is suited for counting things without any regard for fractional parts; integer constants cannot represent fractional parts and integer variables cannot accommodate fractional parts. Practically all computers can accommodate real values that are considerably larger than the largest manageable integers, although these can be substantial. In many instances, whole-number reals can be used instead of integers, so it is quite possible to do considerable programming in Fortran without becoming sensitive to the difference between real and integer modes. Moreover, some Fortrans are forgiving with respect to an occasional change from one to the other, although lots of good programmers resent such laxity. Be guided by their concern. As a first step, resolve to establish and maintain the difference between real and integer in your own thinking.

Perhaps integer variables and integer constants should have been introduced before reals, because integers correspond so closely to the way humans first did their counting, and in this little old world of ours there are a great many whole things to be counted. But most of us have been working and thinking in terms of fractional parts and decimal arithmetic for so long that decimal numbers seem more natural than natural numbers.

Most beginners need practice in distinguishing between Fortran's major types and in remembering that no decimal fraction is associated with either an integer variable or an integer constant. Perhaps the following representation will help. Here the arrows serve to show the permissible combinations of the four words: real, integer, variable, and constant.

Type	*Element*
Real	Variable
Integer	Constant

For example, we recognize real constant (e.g., 36.45) and real variable (e.g., ABQ35). Identification of the first is assured by the presence of the decimal point; the second, because the name begins with the letter A. The word combination "integer constant" refers to a group of numbers without a decimal point, and the combination "integer variable" refers to a name beginning with a letter in the range I–N. We would not expect to do business with a variable constant, and, in the sense the words are used in Fortran, one would shun real integers.

1.13 Integers

The habitual inclination we have developed toward decimal arithmetic can complicate some otherwise simple situations. For instance, a bias toward decimal thinking can obscure the essential characteristic of integers and their proper role in Fortran programming. For emphasis, this characteristic will be noted three ways.

1. The values represented by integer constants and the values taken on by integer variables are **integers**. The set of integers consists of all the natural (counting) numbers, both positive and negative, and zero.

2. **No decimal points** are associated with the values of integer constants or with values taken on by integer variables.

3. **No decimal fraction parts** are associated with the values of integer constants or with the values taken on by integer variables.

You are probably wondering why anyone would make such a big fuss about something so obvious. There are two reasons. First, some unexpected things happen when you program integer operations. Second, although of lessening concern when using contemporary compilers, hazards of varying severity can infect the work of programmers who carelessly mix real and integer types in the same Fortran operation. Lots of skilled practitioners regard Fortran's willingness to accept both integer and real types in the same operation to constitute a major hazard, a potential trap to ensnare unwary programmers in ways that are difficult to detect. They point to newer computer languages that are steadfast in their refusal to attempt any operation that mixes types as indication of the way Fortran should be. They note too that Fortran will not permit mixing of any data types other than real and integer. Some other programmers regard the lack of rigid demarcation between the types integer and real to be a mixed blessing, a hazard to be sure, but not infrequently expeditious for getting jobs done. You will just have to make up your own mind in this regard. But be forewarned: Fortran will permit you to go astray. And your previous experience programming in Basic, or with hand-held calculators won't provide much protection; both are oblivious to the distinction between real and integer.

1.14 Integer Variables

Each Fortran variable name starts with a letter, and it is the first letter in the name that establishes the variable type. Remember, **type** establishes the nature of the data that the variable can accommodate. In Fortran, the letters I, J, K, L, M, and N are used to begin names of variables we will recognize as **integer type** or **integer mode**. Selection of the other characters in the name has no effect on the variable type. For example, KAS would be a serviceable name for an integer variable, and A6K is still a good name for a real variable.

1.15 Integer Arithmetic

Some interesting things happen when arithmetic operations are performed with integers. For example, the segment:

```
K1  =  5
K2  =  K1/6
```

yields the value 0 for variable K2. This is because each integer operation must yield an integer. We say the result is **truncated**; this means that the decimal point and any decimal fraction part, which you might expect to be present in the result, are simply thrown away. With a little coaching most people can get used to this. But when they see:

```
K  =  6+7*2**2*(3/4)
```

their addiction to decimal arithmetic takes over, and they overlook the essential characteristic of integer mode. They start thinking of (3/4) as equal to something like 0.75. It is surprising to see some of the program complications that can result from such misinterpretations. When programming with integers, do your best to keep the essential characteristic of integers in focus. Keep thinking: an integer is an integer is an integer. Also, do your best to program mode- or type-consistent operations. If, for a particular operation, integer mode best serves your purpose, then use it, but be consistent throughout the operation. Try to refrain from indiscriminately using integer and real elements together in the same Fortran operation.

1.16 Exponentiation with Integers

Using both real and integer operations occasionally presents opportunities for fouling up an otherwise flawless program. One is in regard to exponentiation. As noted previously the standard operational symbol for exponentiation is the double asterisk. For example, as long as real variable R has a positive value, RSQ=R**2.0 computes the square of whatever value variable R has and assigns the value to variable RSQ. The example operation is consistent in mode, but, when raising a real to a whole-number power, the form RSQ=R**2 is preferred. Most of us would expect the use of integer 2 with the real variable R to yield one of those mixed-type operations we were all going to avoid. But the integer exponent is accepted by all compilers without a murmur. So, you can raise a positive real value to either a real or an integer power.

Compilers are not so tolerant when exponentiating negative values or integers. The instruction IRS=IR**2.0 spells trouble in most Fortrans. So, raise negative values and integers only with integer exponents. And remember the easy way out when you want whole-number powers. The easy way is to multiply. For instance, RCUBE=R*R*R is usually quicker and cheaper than exponentiating.

1.17 Looping Operations I

When a compiled program is executed, the sequence of events corresponds closely to the sequence of statements in the program. Although it may be an over-simplification, we say that the statements are executed in their order of appearance in the program. After each operation is completed, a result is assigned to a variable. Then control effectively passes to the next instruction in the program, yielding an unbroken sequence of operations. This may be regarded as the most basic transfer of program control. Programs using only this sequential transfer of control unfortunately would be long, not very powerful, and boring to prepare. Perhaps you sensed this while doing one of the early programming exercises. Instead of programming a sequence of statements that is practically the same as an earlier sequence, you may well have wondered why you couldn't arrange to have the same instructions executed again and again. Indeed, why not? This line of thought leads unerringly to the programming of **loops**, sections of program instructions that are to be executed more than once. Until programmers begin to use loops, they miss using the greatest of the computer's capabilities, and much of the fun in programming.

1.18 Fortran's DO

The Fortran DO instruction provides a convenient means for controlling looping operations. In its elementary form, an initial DO is followed by an integer number which also appears later in the program as a statement number. In the examples that follow, these statement numbers are shown ending in column 5, always leaving the column 6 position blank. Further, although it isn't absolutely essential, the numbered

statements used for illustration will all be **CONTINUE** statements. These CON-
TINUEs do not contribute significantly to any program's function; they serve here
only as termination points for the statements that come under the influence of the DO.
In Fortran the programmer can choose practically any number to link a DO and its
CONTINUE together, as long as the same number does not appear as a statement
number on more than one statement. Furthermore, to show how forgiving Fortran
can be, statement numbers need not be in numerical order as they appear in the
program. The DO, and all the statements down to and including the CONTINUE, are
affectionately referred to as a **DO loop**. In skeleton form the loop can be represented:

```
C THIS EXAMPLE SHOWS JUST THE SKELETON OF THE DO LOOP. THE STATEMENTS
C WITHIN THE LOOP ARE NOT SHOWN. THEY ARE REPRESENTED BY THE TWO DOTS.
C
C THE EXAMPLE ALSO INTRODUCES THE USE OF PROGRAM COMMENTS. WHENEVER A
C LETTER C (OR AN *) APPEARS IN THE FIRST COLUMN OF A ROW, THEN THE
C INFORMATION IN THE ROW IS REGARDED AS A COMMENT. COMMENTS SERVE TO
C IDENTIFY YOUR PROGRAM AND ITS PURPOSE, AND PROVIDE CLUES REGARDING
C THE INTENDED FUNCTION OF DIFFERENT SECTIONS OF PROGRAM INSTRUCTIONS.
C
C BLANK COMMENT LINES MAKE PROGRAM COMMENTS MORE NOTICEABLE AND
C READABLE.
C
      DO 66 M = 1,10
      .
      .                        This is the DO loop.
   66 CONTINUE
      .
```

The DO statement, including the integer next-following (for example, the 66)
together with the CONTINUE having the same integer as its **statement number**,
serve to determine the range of program instructions that will be affected by the DO's
presence. The integer variable next-following the DO (in this case, the M) serves as
the **control variable** or **loop index** for the DO. In this example, variable M is to take
on values from 1 to 10; that is what the 1,10 signifies. For each value assumed by M,
all the instructions down to the CONTINUE are to be executed. First, they will be
done with M set equal to 1. Then they will be repeated with M = 2, next with M = 3,
and so on. After all the instructions in the loop have been done the tenth time, control
passes from the CONTINUE to the next statement in the program. This condition is
referred to as normal exit, or exit from the **bottom** of the loop.

The next example shows how some simple operations can be included within a
loop. The control of the loop is maintained by integer variable L. As shown here, the
control variable doesn't have to take part in the operations inside the loop, it just controls the number of times the loop is to be repeated. Take care to note further that the
number 6, appearing just following the DO, and the numbers 1 and 8 have nothing to
do with the number of Fortran instructions contained within the loop. All the instructions after the DO and down to the statement with 6 as its statement number will be
executed; in this example they are to be executed eight times. Before the loop is
entered the constant zero is assigned to variables ANUM and ASUM; if values were

not established for these variables they would not be accepted in the operations following.

The first instruction within the loop increments the value of ANUM by one. The second instruction augments the value of ASUM by whatever value ANUM has. The two instructions together with the PRINT* will be executed eight times.

```
C
C DO LOOP TO PRINT OUT NUMBERS FROM 1.0 TO 8.0
C TOGETHER WITH CUMULATIVE SUMS
C
      ANUM = 0.0
      ASUM = 0.0
      DO 6 L = 1,8
         ANUM = ANUM + 1.0
         ASUM = ASUM + ANUM
         PRINT*, ANUM, ASUM
    6 CONTINUE
      END
```

If you have any doubts regarding the way the DO loop works, then you will probably benefit from running this example program. First, get it to go in the form shown, then try making some changes. Try increasing the upper limit for the control variable. Then change the increment for ANUM from 1.0 to 3.0 or 4.0; operation of the program will then resemble our efforts of years ago when we learned to count by threes and by fours.

When you begin using DO loops, there are a couple of points to remember. The most important is: Do not attempt to manipulate the loop index while control resides inside the loop. DOs are extremely jealous and resent any meddling with their indices. If you need a value that is in some way related to the loop index, assign the index value to another variable and use that variable for your other purposes. As soon as a DO is through, the record of the control variable is lost, so never count on a loop index having a particular value after exit. Feel free to use the same variable to control a subsequent loop if you wish.

The following example program illustrates some of the DO's benefits. It will yield the squares, cubes, and fourth powers of the integers from 1 to 20.

```
C PROGRAM USING A DO LOOP TO FORM AND PRINT OUT
C THE SQUARES, CUBES, ETC. OF INTEGERS FROM 1 TO 20
C
      DO 9 K = 1,20
         N = K
         NSQR = N * N
         NCUBE = NSQR * N
         NFRTH = NCUBE * N
         PRINT*, N, NSQR, NCUBE, NFRTH
    9 CONTINUE
      END
```

This example shows a DO at work, directing the execution of the five statements within the loop to be done twenty times. The control variable K manages all this as it takes on values from 1 to 20. If all this is perfectly clear, there are a few ancillary points that deserve your attention.

1. Note that the five statements within the loop are indented a bit. This leaves the DO lined up in the same column as its CONTINUE and makes the extent of the loop evident at a glance. Of course, the Fortran compiler couldn't care less about this indenting, but it adds a touch of class to your program and eases human interpretation of the program.

2. Observe that the loop index is **not** used in the computations that take place within the loop. Each time through, the current index value is assigned to another variable, N, and it is used in the computations. True, the program would work just as well if the loop index itself were used in the computations. But habit is a powerful influence, and a splendid habit to develop is to refrain from using the index in computations within the loop.

3. Select variable names that suggest the functions of the variables in the program. Those of us who never learned to type frequently tend to use short and unduly cryptic names for our variables. Such practice doesn't necessarily lead to disaster, but it can make human interpretation of a program unduly difficult. At one time the practice recommended here was referred to as using **mnemonic** variable names. Somehow the word never caught on among computer buffs, but go ahead and use mnemonic variable names anyway; they will help you remember what's going on in your program.

1.19 Labeling with Free-Format

Although some worthwhile purposes can be served by programs that yield only numerical results from one or more computations, few but the most insensitive programmers are long satisfied by such bare-bones output. We can identify different output elements more easily and confidently by attaching an appropriate label to each numerical value produced, or by arranging output in columns and heading these with labels. The labeling enabled by the PRINT* instruction is adequate for many purposes. Because this instruction is relatively simple, its use is recommended for the early efforts of programmers who want to identify the different numerical values produced by their programs. When using PRINT*, the label for an individual output item is simply included within apostrophes, or single quote marks, in the list of variables. For example, in a program in which a value of pressure had been computed and assigned to the variable PRESS, most doubts regarding the output could be resolved with the instruction:

```
PRINT*, ' PRESSURE = ',PRESS, 'LBS PER SQUARE INCH'
```

In this example, labels are to be provided in the same output row as the numerical value for the variable PRESS. The label PRESSURE = appears within quotes in the PRINT* instruction, just as it will appear in the output. Of course, the value that has been established for the variable PRESS will appear in the standard, free-format field for real values, between the two labels. In the form shown, the label LBS PER SQUARE INCH may be located too close to the numerical value. The label can be effectively moved to the right by including blank spaces within the quotation mark ahead of the LBS.

When programming for the output of labels to be used for column headings, or in other situations in which only the labels are desired, no variable appears in the PRINT* instruction. For example, the column headings for a simple table of trigonometric functions could be produced with:

```
PRINT*,'    ANGLE        SINE        COSINE '
```

Here the PRINT* produces only the headings, presumably to appear above the columns of values. Of course we should realize that, used this way, the PRINT* instruction is to be executed only once, before entering the loop that grinds out the numerical values.

Two limiting cases deserve consideration. The first is the PRINT* instruction that does not include any label or variable. In such use, the PRINT* instruction yields blank rows in the output. These are useful in locating output rows and in giving emphasis to other rows. The other case is encountered when the labels, or the combination of labels and variables, in the PRINT* instruction become too long to fit within the bounds imposed by columns 7 to 72. As you would no doubt expect, Fortran provides for the continuation of lengthy labels or label-variable combinations. Whenever a nonzero character appears in the column 6 position in a row, that row is regarded as a continuation of the preceding row. For the present, use Fortran's continuation capability sparingly because any attempt to produce a label-variable combination that is too long may crash the program. And do your best to distinguish between the continuation of lengthy labels, or instructions on successive program lines, and the similarly named Fortran instruction CONTINUE. Continuation and more compact means for labeling output are considered in more detail later in a section on formatted output. Meanwhile, if need arises, check the example on page 35.

1.20 Exercises 1-2

Integer arithmetic and looping operations provide the focus for the next exercise set. Start by introducing either, or both of these features into one of your solutions to a previous exercise. For example alter the program you prepared for the first exercise in set 1–1, but now do all operations using integer variables and integer constants; chances are that you will detect some differences in the results. Next, use a loop to produce the multiplication table, or for computing circular areas and spherical volumes. Then try augmenting your handiwork by providing labels to identify each element of output from your program.

1. Run a program that generates factorials but this time use a loop. You may have to provide for factorial zero (0!=1) before setting up the loop. Have your program compute factorials in both integer and real, but be **sure** to keep your computations mode-consistent; do not use integers and reals together in the same operation. Observe the largest factorial for which the real and the integer computation agree and confirm the fact that your machine can deal with much larger factorials when working in real mode.

2. Run a program that evaluates the following expression:

$$(2ab + 3b^2 + b) / (a^2b^3 - 368)$$

   for a = 5 and b = 12. Have your program print the answer in both decimal and fractional form and provide suitable labels for each. (Spencer)

3. Run a looping program that will extend the sequence used in exercise 1.11–10. Determine the amount of error and the percent error when using 1000 and when using 2000 terms in the sequence. Use 3.14159 for your reference, provide suitable labels to identify all results.

4. The lengths of the adjacent and the opposite legs of a right triangle are 4 and 7 respectively. Run a program that computes all six trigonometric functions of the angle opposite the longer leg. Print each value out properly labeled. (Spencer)

5. Run a program that will produce a table with the integers from 1 to 50 in the first column. In the second column list the sums of the numbers in the first column. In the third column put the squares of the numbers from column one. In columns 4 to 6 show the sum of the squares, then the cubes of the numbers from column one, and finally the sums of the cubes. Head the columns with appropriate titles.

6. Run a program that will produce a table of values of the square root of (n*p*q) in which n ranges from 1 to 20 and p has values from 0.1 to 0.5; in each instance q = 1.0 – p. Use exponentiation to the 0.5 power to get the square roots. A table at hand provides the value 1.8330 for p = 0.30 and n = 16.

7. Explore the limits of your computer's ability to accommodate both integers and reals by running parallel computations, one in integer and the other in real mode. Initialize an integer variable to 1 and a real variable to 1.0 then program a loop that multiplies both variables by say, 9. Print out the values of both variables at each iteration of the loop and check the output for signs of change and signs of possible distress. Chances are the output from the real computation will change first to exponential form. Next the integer will show irregular order in size, or an occasional negative sign. At some point either the integer or the real output may stop. Try the looping multiplications with different

multipliers. Estimate the greatest integer and the greatest real value that can be accommodated.

8. Extend the exploration of your system's limits by running a looping program that performs an integer multiplication at each iteration, similar to the previous exercise. Run the loop until the integer products show undeniable evidence of trouble; the evidence may be the appearance of an error or overflow message or the appearance of letters or negative numbers, or simply nothing printed out beyond a certain value. Next run the program but terminate the loop at the iteration before trouble appears and extend your program with a second loop that adds a large integer to the largest valid product produced by the first loop. Extend the second loop until trouble reappears. Then terminate the second loop at one lower iteration and add a third loop that will add a smaller integer to the last valid result from the second loop. Extend your program in this way until you can identify your systems maximum integer or *maxint*. If one is added to maxint the signs of system distress will reappear.

9. One way to obtain the square root of a number is first to assume a value for the root then divide the assumed value into the number. If the resulting quotient is the same as the assumed value, then the job is done; but unless one is very lucky or very shrewd the two will not be the same and further steps are needed. Next use the average of the assumed value and the quotient as the assumed value was first used; divide the average into the number forming a new quotient. Keep on forming a new average using the new quotient and the old average, then dividing the new average into the number until the new quotient and the old average are close enough to regard as equal. Each new average will approach the desired root more closely. Try your program with numbers greater than one and with others less than one, but don't let your numbers get too much less than one!

10. Select a familiar chemical element, say, copper or gold. Think of a single atom of the element. Then think about the mass of the atom expressed as follows:

in amu (atomic mass units)	in kilograms
in grams mass	in pounds mass

Now for the good part. Run a program that will loop 100 times, each time increasing the number of atoms by a factor of ten (1, 10, 100, 1000, etc). Have the number of atoms printed out in the first column and the other information in following columns of output similar to that shown here. Print out suitable column headings and be sensitive to the limit that Fortran's INTEGER type may impose on your efforts.

Number of atoms	Mass in amu	Mass in grams	Mass in kilograms	Mass in pounds
1	63.54	1.055E-22	1.055E-25	2.236E-25
10	635.40	—	—	—
100	—	—	—	—

1.21 Conditional Execution

Consideration is directed next to programming for situations in which the execution of a particular statement may or may not be desired, depending on some condition. The Fortran IF statement provides the key for such programming. IF arranges to test the condition, then branches one way if the condition tests true, the other way if the condition tests false. To make the IF work you will need to know how the conditions are represented; the essential details will be encountered in the next section. For the moment focus on the idea that, at a particular point in the execution of a program, a condition can be true or false. In particular here a variable A can have a value that is less than 100.0.

As it will appear in your programs, the IF is followed by a set of parentheses. The condition to be tested is represented there within the parens. And the statement to be executed, when the condition is true, is situated just following the close parenthesis, all on the same line with the IF. Whenever the condition is found to be false, the executable part is simply ignored, and program control passes without hesitation to the statement in sequence after the IF. For example:

```
.
IF ( A .LT. 100.0 ) A = A + 1.0
.
```

You can see the representation of the condition inside the set of parens; but get the big picture first. Whatever the condition, if it is true then the value of variable A will be increased by one, as directed by the executable part that concludes the statement. After A's value has been incremented, control transfers to the program statement (not shown) next following the IF. When the condition tested is false, the part incrementing variable A is ignored and control passes directly to the program statement next following the IF. As you will see, practically any single executable part can be used to complete the IF.

In the current example the comparison is to be made between the value held by variable A and the real constant 100.0. The .LT. effectively raises a question: "Is the current value of variable A less than 100.0?" The four-character symbol .LT. is the **relational operator** directing the desired comparison. Now, at the instant the statement is encountered during execution, the value held by variable A either **is** less than 100.0 or it **is not** less than 100.0. If the value is less than 100.0, the answer to the question is **yes**. The condition will be regarded as **true**, and the executable part that completes the instruction swings into action. If the value of A **is not** less than that of the constant, then the answer to the question is **no**, the condition is regarded as **false**, and the executable part incrementing A is ignored. The form shown in this example will be referred to as the standard **logical** or **two-branch** IF.

1.22 Relational Operators

The .LT. operator in the last example is one of a set of six. Unless you are a miserable detective, you can decipher these with reasonable confidence. In case of doubt, refer to Table 1. Remember the two dots are part of each operation symbol.

Table 1. Relational Operators

Operation symbol	Meaning
.LT.	Less than
.GT.	Greater than
.LE.	Less than or equal to
.GE.	Greater than or equal to
.EQ.	Equal to
.NE.	Not equal to

Any of these operators can be used with a Fortran IF in the manner shown in the last example. The directed comparison can be between a variable and a constant, or between two variables. Of course, you will be careful to make comparisons that are consistent in type. Compare reals to reals and integers to integers. Check over two more example IFs to emblazon all this in your memory.

```
IF ( S .LT. 1.0E-04 ) S = 1.0E-04
```

Here the current value of real variable S is to be compared to the constant 0.0001. Whenever S's value drops below the designated amount, it will be assigned the value of the constant. No doubt you noticed the sneaky way of representing the small, real constant. The E–04 represents 10 to the –4 power as a factor. Quite right, there is no asterisk in there between the 1.0 and the E; the number and the E-part go together to designate the constant. This example statement is reminiscent of another era. Once upon a time each division programmed had to be preceded by a check to make sure the divisor was not zero. The present IF would serve, provided the values for S were always positive. If this gets you thinking about a way to determine absolute values, rest assured one will be coming along soon.

The next example features two items, a different relational operator and a new Fortran instruction. Obviously the instruction is STOP:

```
IF ( L .EQ. 101 ) STOP
```

The STOP instruction may not seem all that serviceable, but prudent programmers sometimes protect against things getting worse, after they have become bad enough. That's where the STOP comes into play. In the present instance we may surmise that the value of variable L was expected to remain in the range below 100. Evidently, if the value advances to equal 101, there is no point in pursuing the matter further, hence the STOP. The STOP doesn't have to be part of an IF, of course; you can use STOP by itself as a program instruction. We say it is an executable instruction that terminates execution. Some programmers favor inclusion of a STOP in every program, usually close to the END. For your early efforts the STOP will likely be optional, but try to distinguish the jobs done by STOP and END. Remember, the END is a signal to the compiler that there are no more program instructions to be translated.

In the great majority of applications the relational operators behave just as one would expect them to. Nevertheless there may be occasions in which your straightforward programming efforts produce evidence of distress. For example, one implementation of Fortran never misses an opportunity to flash the warning:

```
CAUTION_____IS FLOATING POINT EQUALITY EXPECTED ?
```

This happens whenever a test is made using the .EQ. operator for a comparison between **reals**. Now there are two items for your consideration here. First is to realize that *FLOATING POINT* is the old designation for the data type we now designate as *real*. This goes along with *FIXED POINT* the designation that used to be applied to the data type we now identify as *integer*. But enough history, the root of the problem here is that some decimal (base 10) numbers can not be **exactly** converted to binary. Even though we don't have to become involved with binary operations ourselves, we live with the realization that our computers do their work in binary arithmetic. Granted the aforegoing, it follows that any test for one real being strictly equal to another will **test true only by chance**. Lots of otherwise sagacious students have difficulty incorporating the impact of all this into their thinking. They blithely program IF(A .EQ. 10.0), for example, never suspecting that only infrequently will the test yield a true result when A is truly equal to 10.0, and occasionally will yield a true result when, in fact the two real quantities are not equal. So refrain from programming tests for equality between real quantities. Instead subtract the smaller from the larger and test the difference against an arbitrarily small constant. After all, if the difference between two real quantities is less than 1.0E–06, for a great many purposes the two quantities can be regarded as equal. But be sure you subtract the smaller of the two reals from the larger, or else plan on using the absolute value function to be introduced shortly. If doubt remains, check the example on page 65.

1.23 Reading with Free-Format

In the customary routine of learning a native language, most of us first become involved in using the language in conversational mode. There follows a period, quite painful for some of us, of learning to read. Only after some minimal skill has been established in conversation and reading do we advance to writing. This ordering is reflected in our educational folklore, for example, in the first two items in *readin'*, *'ritin'*, *and 'rithmetic*. When considering the learning of a computer language, the familiar sequence appears to run the wrong way. The business of writing, or printing, is obviously essential to any purposeful computer program. Accordingly, the matter of obtaining computer output has been considered in some detail, whereas nothing has yet been said about reading in data.

The fact is, a substantial amount of programming can be done using only values that are assigned to variables within the program. But programs produced in this way present problems, for instance, when the same computation is to be repeated for several different sets of data. Here the programmer must dig into the program, change the statements in which the values are assigned, and then rerun the program. Before you did this many times, you would realize that there must be a better way. A better way is to program a READ* instruction to obtain a set of values from a data file and effectively assign the values to appropriate variables. The programmed computation is then performed and the initial results printed out. Now the program can loop back to the READ*, read a new set of values into the same variables, and repeat the data processing operations. The values to be read in are separate from the program and can be changed as many times as we please without changing the program.

Most beginners will find free-format a boon for their first efforts to program reading. When arranging data in a file or when entering data values via the terminal keyboard, the individual values are simply separated by blanks. The free-format, or list-directed, READ* searches along a row, gobbling up a separate value for each variable. We speak of the set of variables completing the READ* as a list of variables, hence the alternative term list-directed. If sufficient values are not found on one row, the READ* instruction effectively moves on to the next row of data. Here the READ* is not satisfied by the data found in the first row. If sufficient values are not entered through the keyboard, further action is suspended. If sufficient values are not found in a data file, the READ* remains unsatisfied and a program crash is likely. Attempting to read past the end of a data file in this way is one of the most popular execution-time errors for beginning programmers. Some consideration of the following example may ease the way for those seeking to incorporate READ* instructions into their programs.

```
C
C SKELETON PROGRAM INCLUDING READ*
C
      DO 10 KR = 1,5
      READ*, A, B, C
C
C THE NEXT STATEMENT ECHOES THE DATA
C
      PRINT*, A, B, C
C
C THE NEXT STATEMENT STOPS EXECUTION WHEN A VALUE
C GREATER THAN 1000.0 HAS BEEN READ INTO VARIABLE A
C
      IF (A .GT. 1000.0) STOP
      .
```

Computation and PRINT* statements go in here.

```
C
C NOW CONTROL LOOPS BACK AND THE READING DONE AGAIN
C
   10 CONTINUE
      END
```

Data as arranged in data file or entered via terminal keyboard.

```
   23.6    3.2    9.8
   25.1    3.0    9.8
   27.7    2.8    9.8
 1001.0    0.0    0.0
```

This example program has been stripped down to focus attention on the statements that relate to the READ*. Evidently the READ* is in a loop set up to be traversed five times. The first time through the loop, the three data values in the first row will be read in. The 23.6 will be effectively assigned to variable A, 3.2 to B, and so on. Inasmuch as there are three variables in the list and three values in the first row in the data file, the READ* is satisfied and control transfers to the next program instruction. As indicated in the comment, the next executable statement prints out the values that have just been read in. This is referred to as **echoing** the data. Such echoing enables us to verify that the values were entered as intended. Echoing data is earnestly recommended for all programmers, not just beginners. Echoing is especially appropriate during initial checkout of a program.

The next program statement, the IF, will invoke the STOP whenever a **sentinel**, here a value larger than 1000.0, is detected as the value of variable A. Whenever the value read in for A does not cause the STOP, the block of statements indicated next is executed. All the desired computations are done with the first set of data and the results are printed out. Then program control loops back and the READ* instruction is executed again. The second row in the data file is read in; variable A gets the 25.1, B the 3.0, etc.; the loop is traversed a second time, and a second set of results printed out. The looping continues, performing the computations for a third time and producing output from the last data to be processed.

The fourth time the READ* instruction is executed, variable A gets the sentinel value. The sentinel value, along with zero values for B and C, will be echoed before the STOP instruction takes over. If we objected to having the sentinel value echoed, the echo PRINT* could be moved to a position following the IF.

If the original data were replaced with those shown next, some different events would unfold.

```
   36.4    1.9    9.8
   42.1    1.4    9.8    44.6
           1.2    9.8    48.3
           1.1    9.8
 1001.0
```

Well, the first two trips through the loop will be different only in the values processed. But notice carefully, when the second row of data is read in, the value 44.6 is ignored! This is because the READ* instruction is satisfied by the first three values in the row. Inasmuch as there are only three variables in the READ* list, no more than three values will be considered. Remember, it is the list of variables in the READ* that controls, not the data file. Whenever insufficient data are found, the READ* keeps looking; as soon as the READ* is satisfied, it quits. When subsequently executed, the READ* instruction always moves to a new data line. So, no matter how many extra values appear in a row of data, they are all ignored.

The third time the READ* is executed, the values obtained are 1.2, 9.8, and 48.3. When the fourth data row is read, A and B receive values of 1.1 and 9.8. The value that was evidently intended to provide the sentinel value to variable A is read instead into variable C. We may well presume that the results of ensuing computations will be starkly different from those expected, but that isn't all. The READ* instruction will try to execute once more, but all the data are gone. As you probably guessed, execution is terminated with a tart note saying something about an attempt to read past the end of the data file. This is one way to terminate execution, but not a particularly elegant way.

1.24 Block IF

In some circumstances the control provided by the regular IF leads to clumsy programming. This is evident in a well-worn programming exercise in which numbers, originally in haphazard order, are to be sorted into ascending order. A scheme that is frequently advocated starts by examining successive pairs of entries. If the two values in a pair are in the desired order, attention is shifted to the next pair. If any two values are not in the desired order, the values are interchanged.

To see how the prescribed sorting scheme operates, consider the haphazardly ordered sequence:

    3.6   5.8   1.2   9.1

If these were established as the values for variables A1, A2, A3, and A4, then the first comparison is to be made between the values held by A1 and A2. Since we aim to arrange the numbers in ascending order, there appears to be no reason for interchanging here. The 3.6 is less than the 5.8, so these values are in the desired order, and attention is shifted to the next pair of variables, A2 and A3. The numbers assigned to these variables, the 5.8 and the 1.2, are not properly ordered, so the values are to be interchanged. The interchange results in the transfer of the value that A3 held initially to A2, and the transfer of A2's value to variable A3. If, after the interchange, we printed out the variables in the same order, the sequence of values would appear as:

    3.6   1.2   5.8   9.1

A third comparison, now between the 5.8 and the 9.1, shows them to be in the proper order, so no further interchange is indicated.

Now the entire sequence of comparisons must be made again. The interchange leaves an adjacent pair that has not been checked for the desired order. To assure the desired ordering of all four values, we must repeat the three comparisons three times. This provides for the worst case: when the smallest value must be moved from the last position all the way to first.

Those stalwarts who try programming the sorting of even so modest a number of values in this way, using just Fortran's regular, two-branch IF, may well experience malaise. Why not try this as an exercise? After all, a little malaise never hurt anyone. Moreover, if you do this, you will better appreciate the convenience afforded by a modest extension of the regular IF the **block IF**.

The block IF directs the execution of practically any number of statements, again depending on the outcome of some comparison. The comparison works just the same way, but *THEN* appears in place of the executable part of the ordinary IF. Practically any number of executable statements can follow an IF thus embellished with THEN. Most agree it is a great convenience to be able to control such a group, or block, of statements depending on only one comparison. Of course, we pay a price for all the convenience. This time it is to remember that ENDIF must follow the block of executable statements. All this will become perfectly clear from the next example, although to make sure the desired result is obtained, perhaps you should complete and run the whole thing.

```
C
C INCOMPLETE PROGRAM FOR SORTING FOUR NUMBERS USING THE
C    * * *  BLOCK IF  * * *
C
C READ IN THE VALUES IN HAPHAZARD ORDER
C
      READ*, A1, A2, A3, A4
C
C COMPARE THE FIRST AND SECOND VALUES.  IF THEY ARE NOT
C IN THE DESIRED ORDER , THEN INTERCHANGE THE VALUES
      .
      IF (A1 .GT. A2) THEN
         TEMP = A1
         A1 = A2
         A2 = TEMP
      ENDIF
C
C A SECOND COMPARISON WITH A SECOND BLOCK
C
      IF (A2 .GT. A3) THEN
         TEMP = A2
         A2 = A3
         A3 = TEMP
      ENDIF
      .
```

To guide you on your way to the completion of the intended program, note first the location of each THEN and its companion ENDIF. The THEN stands in place of the single executable in the ordinary IF. Each ENDIF appears following a block of executable statements, lined up columnwise with the IF to which the ENDIF belongs. If you are becoming sensitive to programming style, you will appreciate the indentation of the statements within each block; this emphasizes their "togetherness." Of course, whenever the condition tested is found to be false, the whole block is skipped.

Why not flesh out the program and make it work with a set of different values? Think how you could adapt your efforts to sorting a larger batch of numbers. Then try the same task without the block IF or **IF-THEN-ENDIF**, as it is sometimes called.

Both the capacity for looping, which the DO provides, and the ability to program conditional execution of groups of instructions, which is present in the IF-THEN-ENDIF, offer substantial extensions to any beginner's programming skill. However, as is frequently the case, the new extensions introduce an element of risk. The risk becomes evident in programs that include both the DO and the IF-THEN-ENDIF. But before coming to grips with the potential hazard, let's consider some combinations that work just fine. First, it is eminently permissible to have an IF block inside a DO loop. Why not run the next example and confirm this?

```
C
C PROGRAM TO EXPLORE DO'S AND IF'S
C
      DO 100 IR = 1,10
         IK = IR
         IF (IK .GT. 5) THEN
            J = 5*IK
            PRINT*, IK, J
         ENDIF
         PRINT*,IK
  100 CONTINUE
      END
```

Evidently the range of the DO is to be executed ten times. During the first five of these, the IF-THEN is dormant. After the loop control variable increments to 6, the instructions within the IF block swing into action. Note carefully, though, that the IF block is entirely within the range of the DO.

In a similar vein, it is quite acceptable to have a DO loop within an IF block, as long as it is all within the block. Here the CONTINUE must occur in sequence before the ENDIF. Probably you have begun to suspect the hazard here. Disappointment will almost surely be your lot if either a DO loop is begun within an IF block, but not completed within the block, or if an IF block is begun within the range of a DO, but figuratively sticks out through the bottom of the loop.

1.25 IF-THEN-ELSE

Situations frequently arise in which we want to pursue one or another of two extensive and exclusive courses of action, depending on the outcome of a single decision. The sinking ship decision comes to mind. If the ship we happen to be on is sinking, several prospective actions come to mind: request help, put on a life jacket, locate a lifeboat, etc. If the ship is not sinking, other things can be done: arrange the deck chairs, put new film in the camera, order another round of drinks, etc. Now the counterpart of this real-life situation can be represented in a computer program with two IF-THEN blocks. But by now you just know there is another way. Some enthusiasts refer to the other way introduced here as the **double-alternative decision structure**; others simply name it the **IF-THEN-ELSE-ENDIF**. Whatever you call it, the combination enables compact programming of a great many situations. But before turning to an illustrative example, take time to remember that the more complicated situations can always be programmed with the simpler structures. The double-alternative can be programmed with two of the single-alternative blocks, and indeed, if one prefers, the most involved situations can be reduced to a form accommodated by standard logical IFs. Don't make the mistake of sanctifying program structures simply because they are complicated and powerful. If the simpler structure serves your purpose and you are confident in its use, use it.

```
C
C SIMPLE-MINDED PORTRAYAL OF IF-THEN-ELSE-ENDIF CONTROL
C
      .
      IF (ANGL .GT. 45.0) THEN
          DESIRE = BOATS + OARS
          ALARM = SOS
          HOPE = FLOAT
      ELSE
          REST = CHAIR + SHADE
          DRINK = GIN + ICE
          PICTR = GOOD
      ENDIF
```

In the example at hand we may surmise the angle being tested is the inclination of the deck, and, unless this is a smallish sailing vessel, an angle of greater than 45.0 degrees represents cause for concern. If the condition tested is true, the first block, the THEN block, is executed and the other instructions skipped over. If the condition isn't true, the THEN block is skipped and the other block, the ELSE block, is executed. Chances are this works just as you would expect.

1.26 Library Functions

One does not become deeply involved in programming before the need arises for a square root or perhaps a logarithm. Most of us have been obtaining such items from hand-held calculators for some time by simply touching an appropriate key. Similar capabilities are available for all Fortran programmers in the form of **library functions**. Some refer to them as intrinsic functions, although they are not intrinsic in Fortran. These functions are programs that are supplied with the Fortran compiler. One of them is invoked whenever a recognizable library-function name appears in the operational part of a program statement. For example, there is a library function named SQRT ready to grind out square roots. The function goes to work whenever its name appears, along with a suitable value on which to operate. The term **argument** has been adopted to refer to the thing on which the function is to operate. The argument appears within a set of parens, right after the function name. For example, the program statement:

```
      .
      B = SQRT (5.0)
      .
```

causes a transfer of control to the square root function. The argument value, here 5.0, is taken along. Next the function performs its job; the result is obtained and, together with program control, transferred back to the operation in which the function name appeared. In the jargon of the trade we say the function is **called** from the point in the program at which its name appears. Control is transferred to the function and its job is done. Then the result, along with control, is **returned** to the point at which the function was called. In the sample statement all this is followed by the assignment of the returned value to variable B.

Although we could call the SQRT function using a constant for the argument, as shown in the example, functions are usually called with variables as arguments. For example, the calling statement:

```
.
B = SQRT (A)
.
```

is more typical. Of course, some value must have already been established for variable A by the time the call is made to SQRT. And a moment's reflection will confirm certain limits on argument values. The limits are different for different functions. The SQRT function refuses to do business with negative arguments, for example. ASIN, the function for obtaining arcsines, will become upset with arguments having values outside allowable limits for sines and cosines. Some conventions must also be recognized. For instance, the arguments for all trigonometric functions are interpreted to be in **radians**, not degrees. A few popular library functions are listed in Table 2. In all probability, these and many more are available on the system that serves you.

Table 2. Selected Library Functions

Function name	Common name	Argument note
ABS (A)	Absolute value	Real
ACOS (A)	Arc cosine	ABS(A) .LE. 1.0
ALOG (A)	Natural log	.GE. zero
ALOG10 (A)	Base 10 log	.GE. zero
ASIN(A)	Arcsine	ABS(A) .LE. 1.0
ATAN(A)	Arc tangent	Real
COS (A)	Trigonometric cosine	Real (in radians)
EXP (A)	Exponential (e**A)	Real
IABS (K)	Absolute value	Integer
INT(A)	Integer	Real
MOD(J,K)	Remainder from (J/K)	Integer or real
NINT(A)	Nearest integer	Real
RANF(A) or RAND(A)	Random number	Use 0.0
REAL(K)	Real equivalent of K	Integer
SIN (A)	Trigonometric sine	Real (in radians)
SINH(A)	Hyperbolic sine	Real
SQRT (A)	Square root	.GE. zero
TAN(A)	Trigonometric tangent	Real (in radians)

The ability to program looping or iterative operations, along with the capability provided by library functions, enables production of considerable information that in the past was available only in mathematical tables. The example presented next shows this and also illustrates some of the recently introduced elements of Fortran.

```
C
C THIS PROGRAM WILL PRODUCE A SPECIAL PURPOSE TABLE OF
C TRIGONOMETRIC FUNCTIONS.  THE TABLE LISTS FUNCTION VALUES
C FOR FIVE-DEGREE INCREMENTS OF ANGLE FROM ZERO TO 80.0
C DEGREES, THEN BY ONE DEGREE INCREMENTS FROM 80.0 TO 90.0
C DEGREES. THE SELECTION OF INCREMENT IS MADE WITH A BLOCK
C IF-THEN-ELSE.
C
C PRINT OUT COLUMN HEADINGS FOR THE TABLE
C
      PRINT*,' ANGLE - DEGREES      ANGLE - RADIANS          SIN
     2        COSINE          TANGENT '
      PRINT*,' '
      ANDEG = -5.0
      DO 100 K = 1  ,27
         IF(ANDEG .LT. 80.0) THEN
            ANDEG = ANDEG + 5.0
         ELSE
            ANDEG = ANDEG + 1.0
         ENDIF
         ANRAD = ANDEG * 3.14159/180.0
         SIGN = SIN (ANRAD)
         CSGN = COS (ANRAD)
         TNGT = TAN (ANRAD)
         PRINT*, ANDEG, ANRAD, SIGN, CSGN, TNGT
  100 CONTINUE
      END
```

The example features first a label that is printed out before the loop is entered. In order for the labels to extend over the columns provided by list-directed output the column headings must be positioned by including blank spaces in the literal field bounded by the single quote marks. There are a couple of hazards here. First, as more blank spaces are inserted in the label as it appears in the program, the label becomes longer and the chance increases for some of it to be moved beyond column 72. If this happens then the part of the heading that is pushed to the right beyond column 72 will be lost. Of considerably more concern, the single quote that closes the literal field will also be lost, and this assures a crashed program. The loss of the second quote mark closing the field just won't be tolerated.

The example shows how the loss can be prevented. The program line that contains the first part of the headings is continued on a second row in the program. As shown, the numeral two in column six causes the desired continuation; in the label produced by the program, 'COSINE' will appear on the same line with 'SINE' separated from it by a dozen or so spaces. Beginning programmers will frequently misplace the continuation character, getting it in either column 5 or column 7. Whenever a program line has been continued check carefully to be sure the continuation character is indeed in column six position.

The next feature to consider is the separation of the loop control from the computation performed in the loop. Loop control here is effected by the integer variable K; it is to take on values from 1 to 27 providing the desired number of loop iterations. The computation within the loop is based on variable ANDEG. This variable is initialized to –5.0 before the loop is entered. Then variable ANDEG is incremented by 5.0, so 0.0 is the first value that will be processed. Of course it would be possible to use the control variable in the computation within the loop, although it wouldn't be much help here. And, as you will see later on, we can control DO loops with real variables. Nonetheless, the recommendation here is to use integers for control of loop iterations, and to keep the control of the loop separate from the computations done inside the loop. This course of action will reduce the chance of an inadvertent attempt to change a control variable and just possibly stem the inclination to thoughtlessly mix real and integer in the same operation.

The next matter deserving your notice is the application of the IF-THEN-ELSE to control the amount by which the value of ANDEG is to be incremented. If the condition tested is true, the THEN block is executed and the ELSE block is skipped; the angle is incremented by five degrees. If the condition is found to be false, the THEN block is skipped and the angle is incremented by one degree in the ELSE block. Note, too, the effective conversion from degree measure to radians before invoking the library functions. If you are not presently familiar with radian measure, perhaps a quick refresher in trigonometry would be worthwhile.

1.27 Program Troubles

If you have been doing your part by preparing and running a short program every couple of days, then chances are that you already know about several of the items of concern in this section. Unless you are rather unusual you have already survived the experience of a crashed program. Let's put that another way. If by the time you read this you haven't had difficulty with a program or two, then chances are you haven't been pushing ahead with sufficient vigor. Now it's not that anyone wishes your programs to malfunction nor is trying to get you to make mistakes, although such thoughts may cross your mind occasionally. The fact is, no matter how carefully we prepare, say through practice in translating algebra into Fortran, when the time comes to submit the results of our efforts for compilation most of us discover we have erred a time or two. And most of us find our most intense learning attends the discovery and remediation of our own mistakes. Accordingly an early lesson in programming might well be directed toward attitude adjustment with respect to mistakes. Instead of considering an error message as a rebuke, try to regard it as a challenge. Develop confidence that there is a remedy for the condition presently blocking your efforts and that you will truly be richer having experienced the error and then persevered until the cause discovered and the remedy applied.

Fortunately, very few of us pursue development of programming skill in isolation. Inasmuch as beginners so frequently make mistakes, support services have developed to assist in the virtually inevitable detection and remediation of common programming errors. For example, the chances are good that any program difficulty you have encountered thus far was resolved through the intervention of someone who had encountered the same, or a very similar difficulty before. A considerable amount of information regarding the correction of program troubles is transmitted through the network of persons currently pursuing development of their own skills. One usually finds a mix of skill levels being pursued at any location, so ongoing learning proceeds in ways similar to that in French schools, where the sixth grade students have considerable responsibility for helping the fifth graders, etc.

A second source of assistance for the beginning programmer has been built into every Fortran compiler. Some mistakes have been made so frequently in the past the compilers now have appropriate error messages built-in. Thus, when an inhibiting error is detected by the compiler, it will try to explain the trouble it is having; but it can respond only with one of the error messages with which it has been equipped. Inasmuch as error messages are not standardized, Fortran compilers are not uniform in the ability to explain their troubles—but they all try. So a programmer with a non-functioning program is well advised to search for error messages from the compiler. These may be found with other information printed out either preceding or following the listing of the program, or sometimes within the program listing itself. Sometimes the message is just a number, and reference must be made to a numbered list of error messages. Usually the messages provide clues to the source of trouble but sometimes these clues are so brief, so cryptic, and so well hidden among the other printed output their effectiveness is limited. At other times a great number of error messages may appear, sorely testing the programmer's self-confidence.

Neither instance should cause undue concern. Regard the messages as counsel from a friend. If many errors are noted, address those appearing first. Occasionally a simple error occurring early in a program will yield a veritable cascade of error messages. Under such circumstances the correction of one error often makes many error messages go away. If an error message cannot be found nor deciphered, then one must recruit human help. When seeking human help make a practice of taking along the most recent available listing of the errant program. And don't mark heavily over the program listing, no matter how upset you become; heavy markings can obliterate items essential to effective repair.

Granted, the practical inevitability that each of us will sometimes find the assistance of another person essential to our progress, there are, nonetheless, actions that will reduce the probability of such need. First is to become sensitive to the distinction between **compilation** errors and **execution** errors. As you no doubt recognize by now, irregularities in the program instructions you prepare inhibit the Fortran compiler in its work. Now compilers don't give up easily and if the faults in your work are not too severe, the compiler may issue a word of warning or may even let your transgression go by seemingly unnoticed. Of course, if the problem your program presents to the compiler is too much for it to handle, the message issued will be COMPILATION ABORTED along with a note indicating the line of your program in which the infringement was detected and maybe some additional details. Your course now leads back to the editor and an attempt at making corrections. There may follow a series of program submissions and rejections before all is well from the compiler's point of view. Try to keep from becoming discouraged here, chances are good that if you persevere your efforts will pass the stern tests imposed by your compiler. But after compilation comes execution, and some programs that satisfy the former, don't measure up all that well with the latter. Usually execution errors can be rooted out by programming extra PRINT instructions and painstakingly following through the program step by step. Mind, nobody said this sort of thing is especially enjoyable, they said it usually can be done.

To maintain the likelihood of the success of your programs, give thought to the following errors frequently made by fledgling Fortraners. Try to understand how they can impact your efforts, and resolve to check the results of your work before seeking a compiler's opinion. In a great many instances you'll be glad you did.

1. **Beginning a program statement before column 7, or extending the statement beyond column 72.** This faux pas is frequently found in the work of those of us who never learned to type, because we are looking at the keyboard when we should be paying attention to the screen. If your keyboard skills don't measure up, plan now to double check the limits 7 to 72.

2. **Improper location of the continuation character or of a statement number.** Just remember continuation characters **must** be in column 6 position and statement numbers **must not** extend into column 6 position. Check again the treatment of the long label in the example on page 35. If you have difficulty determining the column positions for the statement numbers and continuation characters in your program files, then insert program comments that consist of decades of numbers. For example either C2345678901 . . . or *2345678901 . . . (beginning in column one and extending to column 72) inserted right there within the file will enable confident identification of columns. Note that either the letter C or the asterisk in column one can be used to start a program comment. These 'numerical comments' can be removed later if you wish.

3. **Unbalanced parentheses.** Go through each statement, count up one for each open and down one for each close paren; the resulting count should be zero. No matter how smart you are, you will find the number of)s must be exactly the same as the number of (s.

4. **Undefined variable.** This one may yield a warning on compilation and/or interrupt program execution; then again it may do neither. But for complete satisfaction every variable appearing in a Fortran operation must already have a value.

5. **Illegal data in field.** Expect this one at execution time if you try to read data including decimal points into an integer variable, or a letter or punctuation mark into either a real or an integer variable. One Fortran at

hand is very helpful; it provides a snippet of the offending data line, and an asterisk right beside the cause of the difficulty. Let's hope your Fortran is as helpful under similar circumstances.

6. **Read past end of data.** For beginners this message usually means the programmer forgot to provide access to the data to satisfy the READ* instruction(s) in the program. More advanced students can get the same message by programming the reading in a loop, but providing data for only the first trip. After receiving the message a time or two you will see the wisdom in **echoing the data**, that is, printing out the values just read in, especially when checking out a new program.

7. **Arithmetic error or dividing by zero.** This difficulty does not present the hazard it once did, but it usually terminates execution. Sometimes the division is permitted, but the trouble comes when attempting to use the value resulting from the division.

8. **Exceeding the time allowed.** This is an old standby for many neophytes. In most instances it means the programmer has inadvertently included an endless loop in the works. Sometimes detection is aided by injecting an extra PRINT or two to see what is going on. Some programmers seem to believe that using WHILE loops (to be featured later) instead of DO loops helps. But don't fall for the line that you can't program an endless WHILE loop.

Now that your attention has been called to a few of the popular ways for crashing a program, see if you can avoid the attendant difficulties as you show your prowess with the following exercises.

1.28 Exercises 1-3

This set of exercises will prompt your use of all the programming skills designated as level one. Some participants may be aware of skills yet to be introduced that will substantially simplify some of the tasks to be done here. The recommendation is for plenty of practice with the elementary skills to get them under good control before moving on. The Immelmann turns will come in due time.

1. Run a program that reads two different integers and prints them out together with the sum of the two plus all integers between the two.

2. Run a program that reads in a substantial group of integers and prints out the total number read, together with a count of the odd and of the even integers in the set.

3. Use the same data set you prepared for the previous exercise. This time read the data into real variables, and then distinguish between odds and evens using REAL computations throughout.

4. Run a program that reads in two different integers. If the difference between the two is an even number, print out all the odd integers

between the two integers read in. If the difference is an odd number, print out all the integers bounded by the two read in.

5. Augment the program produced for exercise 1–2–5 in the following way. First, select two integers at random from the range 100 to 10000, then establish the count of integers in the table produced that fall within the range established by the selected integers.

6. A Pythagorean triple is a set of numbers that satisfies the relationship

$$A^2 + B^2 = C^2$$

The numbers (3, 4, 5) and (5, 12, 13) are Pythagorean triples, as you can readily confirm. Find 12 other sets. (Spencer)

7. Shirts that originally sold for $2.00 were put on sale at Tudburry's haberdashery. The total amount collected from the sale of the shirts was $603.77. Use your recently acquired computer skills to determine the number of shirts sold and the sale price for each.

8. Program production of a range table for a simple projectile. Use launch angles in five degree increments from 10.0 to 45.0 degrees. To utilize free-format, select five different launch speeds. The table produced is to have angles in degrees in the left column with five columns of range values. Each table entry will list the distance the projectile will travel, for example with launch angle of 10.0 degrees and a speed of 100 meters per second, the range is close to 349 meters. After you provide suitable labels for the table modify your program to cover different five- or ten-degree increments in steps of one degree.

9. Prepare a program that reads in the speeds of two runners and the headstart the first runner is given. Have your program compute the time necessary for the second runner to overtake the first, and the distance at which overtaking occurs. If the second runner can't overtake the first, have your program print a suitable message.

10. You have been commissioned by an agricultural entrepreneur to augment his store of livestock. He has given you $1000.00 and told you to buy 100 animals. Your instructions are to spend all the money. At the livestock yard you find cows, sheep, and pigs cost $100, $25, and $5 respectively. How many of each should you buy?

11. Joe is swimming in a river when he has a cramp and calls for help; he is 80 feet from the river bank when the difficulty develops. Al, who is 60 feet upstream at the time, hears the call and goes to the rescue. Al can run 15 miles per hour and swim 6 miles per hour; the river current is negligible. Prepare a program that will assist Al in deciding how far he should run, and how far he should swim in order to get to Joe in the shortest time.

12. Isosceles trapezoids are formed with a 2-inch base and 2-inch slant sides. Prepare a program that loops through a range of angles and find the angle between the base and a slant side that yields maximum trapezoid area. You may find working with the supplement of the internal angle simpler (see diagram).

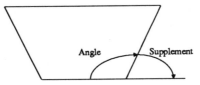

Angle   Supplement

13. Determine the length of the hypotenuse in each of the right triangles shown in the diagram. Determine the number of the triangle, in sequence shown, for which the difference between the hypotenuse and the adjacent side becomes less than 0.05, this is the 'target' triangle. Have your program print out the hypotenuse and adjacent side lengths and the included angle for the target triangle and for the triangle just before and for the triangle just after it in sequence.

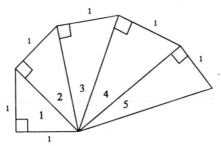

14. The accompanying table represents the output from a program produced with first-level skills. The table provides logarithms for numbers at intervals between 1.00 and 10.00. The table is entered with an argument made up of a value from the left hand column augmented by a value from the top row. For example, the base three log of 2.400 is found to be 0.79968860; this value is found at the intersection of the second row (beginning 2.0) and the fourth column (beginning 0.400). The program is activated by reading in a real value that appears in the table caption and serves as the base for the tabulated logarithms. How about showing the world that you have good control of the first level skills, and a handshaking acquaintance with some fundamentals of algebra, by preparing a program to produce similar output? Check your program with unusual bases, say 0.655 or 17.500. If, from a cold start, you can program for the desired output in 30 minutes, give yourself a resounding pat on the back. If two hours isn't sufficient for you to do the job, chances are you need a bit more practice with simple programs, or maybe you would benefit from a spirited review of algebra—or possibly both.

```
         Short Table of Logarithms to the Base 3.000000
I--------------I-----------------------------------------------------
I  ARGUMENT    I  0.0000000E+00  0.2000000     0.4000000     0.6000000
I--------------I-----------------------------------------------------
I  1.000000    I  0.0000000E+00  0.1659563     0.3062702     0.4278157
I--------------I-----------------------------------------------------
I  2.000000    I  0.6309298      0.7176848     0.7968860     0.8697440
I--------------I-----------------------------------------------------
I  3.000000    I  0.9999999      1.058745      1.113928      1.165956
I--------------I-----------------------------------------------------
I  4.000000    I  1.261860       1.306270      1.348615      1.389076
I--------------I-----------------------------------------------------
I    .         I     .              .             .             .
I--------------I-----------------------------------------------------
I  10.00000    I  2.095903       2.113928      2.131603      2.148942
I--------------I-----------------------------------------------------
```

1.29 Summary for Level One

The skills envisioned here as representing a first identifiable level may be regarded as typical of those attained by a person of average aptitude who has successfully prepared and run four or five short, independent programs. Our level-one practitioner will readily demonstrate job submission and retrieval of output using an accessible computer. In a sense, these skills are not part of Fortran, but are still essential.

The Fortran-related skills to be demonstrated include using types real and integer effectively in programming numerical computation, programming simple loops, conditionally executing single instructions and groups of instructions, using a few library functions, printing out results, and reading in data with free format. Level-one practitioners use Fortran's first-letter, default typing of real and integer variables as they do free-format. Some of them have experienced disenchantment with the limits of free-format, most of them are not yet sensitive to the mixing of reals and integers in the same operation. All have come to value program comments and strive to incorporate them in their programs. Most of them have programmed labels for program output, although with varying levels of success. Conceivably a level-one fledgling could program any possible computation, but lots of these wouldn't be much fun.

Chapter 2

Intermediate Programming Skills

The difference between an engineer and a scientist? Simple! In our society engineers make money; scientists spend it.   —Wm. T. Wood [1]

Only a few of those who use Fortran to unleash the power of a computer will be content with the skills offered here as representing a first level. One doesn't do much programming before the restriction of working only with Fortran's real and integer modes begins to grate. Some relief is at hand in the provision for declaring variables, that is, establishing the variable type as the programmer wishes. Another opportunity for increased programming power lies in the capacity to manipulate character data. Inasmuch as Fortran was developed with special emphasis on numerical computation, manipulation of character data was given short shrift in early versions. In some contrast, contemporary Fortrans have substantial capacity for manipulating character data. But the most significant single advance in the skill of a majority of beginning programmers comes as they develop the ability to use singly subscripted variables. The concepts and the utility of working with arrays first impact the lives of most students as they advance in programming skill; until a measure of related ability is in hand, it is practically impossible for fledgling programmers to grasp the importance subscripted variables hold for their work. Some further consideration of looping and the ability to produce output in the form the programmer wants, rather than in the

---

1.   William T. Wood (1905–1983) obtained his mechanical engineering degree from
    Lafayette College in 1927. He served the E. I. duPont de Nemours & Co. for 42 years.
    In 1964 he was the company's chief engineer.

the programmer wants, rather than in the way free-format dictates, complete the current list of major goals. Incorporating these, with a few minor items thrown in, become the objectives for those aspiring to a second level of programming skill.

2.1 Type Considerations II

When using only REAL and INTEGER, Fortran's two most popular data types, programmers need not specifically declare the variables they intend to use. The A–H, and I–N first-letter convention establishes the type for each variable and, as long as programmers are content with this **implied** or **default** typing, they can jump right in and program away. In most instances, Fortran forgives those of us who occasionally err with respect to data typing. For example, the inadvertent (or advertent) assignment of an integer quantity to a real variable is no cause for concern. If the assignment is made the other way, the real quantity assigned to the integer variable, the compiler may take note and issue a mild word of caution. Of course, if the real value includes a decimal fraction part, this will be lost when the assignment is made to the integer variable. But occasionally this is the intent of the programmer. Most Fortran practitioners do not regard either of these change-of-type assignments as representing mixing of type.

Even when mixing of type is undeniably present in an operation, it may go unnoticed. Some contemporary compilers are almost humble in their willingness to forgive and reluctance to admonish. They just know that, when both INTEGERs and REALs are present in an operation, in all but a vanishingly small percentage of cases the operation simply has to be done in REAL. So why bother? Without a murmur, the compiler makes the needed conversions and the computation is done without the programmer ever being aware of the infraction.

There are two points here for your consideration. First is the fact that Fortran compilers are not uniform in their ability to accommodate, and indeed to protect you against the hazard of mixed mode. So when one carelessly mixes mode in operations he or she invites trouble. The second point is that some programmers feel the first-letter convention unduly restricts their choice of variable names. Some want their programs to be near works of art, and as a result want to use a variable COUNT say as an integer. This all leads to the declaration or specification of variable types. For integers and reals declaration is optional, for other data types it is essential. Declaration enables naming real and integer variables as you like, but try to understand: Delaration in itself provides no whit of protection against possible difficulties stemming from mixed mode operations.

2.2 Type Declaration

The option for declaring enables variables to be established in the type preferred. For example, the two statements:

```
REAL ITEM, LIMIT
INTEGER COUNT, BIG
```

ensure that each of the four variables declared will be regarded in type different from the way we have come to expect. In the program at hand, variable ITEM will be real and COUNT will be integer. To do their job, the declaration statements must be at the beginning of the program.

As will presently become evident, declaration statements can serve program purposes apart from simply establishing variable type. When using Fortran data types other than real and integer, declaration is essential. Undeniably the practice of declaring variables is catching on among discriminating programmers. Perhaps this is in tacit recognition of the requirement imposed by some other programming languages to declare every variable. So why not get started declaring the variables you plan to use in each of your programs? Even though it isn't essential at this level, it adds a nice touch.

2.3 Type Conversion

On occasion we may want to make a change of type, for example, to use the current value of an integer in a real computation. Contemporary Fortran is equipped with four library functions to enable such programming with type-consistent operations. Two of these provide conversion from real to integer, and two provide for conversion the other way. Conversion from integer to real is handled by either of the library functions REAL or FLOAT. In use these function names appear followed by parens enclosing an argument, all in the operation part of a statement. For example, conversion of the contents of integer variable K9 to provide a new value for real variable Z would be done either with Z = REAL(K9), or with Z = FLOAT(K9). The operation parts of these statements could be used as well as the Z in subsequent operations. With these as role models, you can probably guess how functions INT and IFIX would be pressed into service. Arguments for INT and IFIX are real, and the values returned are integer.

2.4 Integer Functions

Fortran provides several library functions which are of special service when programming in the world of INTEGER. In addition to the aforementioned conversion function INT, you might want to try its cousin NINT. This one doesn't always throw away the fractional part of the real argument; it returns the integer nearest to the value of the argument.

If you have used the real function ABS, which produces the absolute value of a real quantity, then you probably can put its integer counterpart to work. IABS(K5) will provide the absolute value of whatever K5 happens to hold. The function MOD requires two integer arguments. MOD proceeds to divide the first argument by the second, and then returns the remainder. For example, MOD(7,3) equals 1. Better check this one out. Last to be introduced are two functions that will fetch the maximum or the minimum values in a list of integers. The name of the first consists of the three characters MAX, with a zero tacked on (MAX0). With this much to go on, you would unerringly recognize the other, MIN0. Put the list of integer variables from which selection is to be made in a set of parens, as in K = MIN0(L1,L2,L3,L4).

2.5 CHARACTER

Of the Fortran data types that must be declared, the first we consider is CHARAC-TER. As you probably expect, the declaration necessarily appears at the beginning of the program, before any executable instructions. The example declaration:

```
CHARACTER NAME*10, TEAM*12, KEY
```

establishes the three named variables as of type CHARACTER. The asterisk and number following a name determine the maximum number of characters which the variable can accommodate. If no number appears with a declared variable, then it can hold only one character. If all the variables declared were to have the same size, the asterisk and an appropriate number would precede the first variable in the declaration list. For example:

```
CHARACTER *15 CLASS, GROUP
```

sets up both CLASS and GROUP as being of the type currently under consideration, and each capable of accommodating 15 Ps or Qs or other characters.

When you program the assignment of a value to a CHARACTER variable, the value assigned must be consistent in type. If you are assigning a constant to one of these variables, make sure it is a CHARACTER constant. The distinction between the desired type and other types is provided by placing all the characters that are to make up the CHARACTER constant within single quotes. The assignment statements:

```
NAME = 'JOHN HANCOCK'
TEAM = 'PANTHERS'
KEY  = '5'
```

establish the evident values for the previously declared variables. The values selected, in combination with the declared size of the variables, illustrate some salient points about CHARACTER operations in Fortran. First, the string 'JOHN HANCOCK' is evidently too big to fit in a variable of size 10. Note the string includes 12 characters. Don't forget that the blank is a character and must be counted. Even your little sister knows the constant can't be crowded into the variable. Now we ask: Which end of the constant is lost, the 'JO' or the 'CK'? Evidently the individual characters get packed into the variable from left to right, so the 'CK' gets left out in the cold. The same scheme is followed in the second assignment. This time the variable is larger than needed. Filling of individual characters proceeds the same way. This leaves the four right-hand locations in the variable TEAM empty; well, they aren't really empty, they get filled in, but with blanks. Finally, with respect to the value assigned to KEY, try to appreciate that the '5' is starkly different from our old friend integer five. Don't ever make the mistake of trying to do ordinary data processing operations with CHARACTER 5s and 5.0s. CHARACTERs are valued for their adornment of our programming efforts. They just won't compute. Furthermore, whereas mixing of integer and real types in Fortran operations is undesirable, mixing of CHARACTER with another type is fatal.

When printed out with free-format, the individual characters in a string appear side by side. Ten spaces along an output row will be needed to accommodate output from a variable declared CHARACTER*10. Note that if the variable has been assigned the constant 'a b c d e ' then there will be ten CHARACTERs in the output, but five of them will be blanks. The quote marks[2] do not appear with the free-format output but they **must** be included around the data to be read into CHARACTER variables. The reason, of course is that inasmuch as a blank is as good a CHARACTER as a letter, we must have the quote mark signaling the beginning of the data. Otherwise, when reading from a data line holding ten blanks followed by your name, the READ* might be satisfied by reading the blanks, and never get around to finding your name.

2.6 Substrings

As you no doubt would expect, substrings are pieces of strings. Fortran enables plucking out parts of strings of characters. Either individual characters or groups of characters can constitute substrings. In the character string 'JOHN HANCOCK', which was assigned to variable NAME, the substring 'OH' can be identified as NAME(2:3). The two numbers in the parens designate the first and last of the string's characters to be included in the substring. If a single-character substring is wanted, the same number appears on both sides of the colon within the parens. For example, NAME(7:7) designates the substring 'A'. When one of the numbers inside the parens is omitted, the reference left out is to the end of the variable. The combination TEAM(:5) refers to 'PANTH', and TEAM(7:) focuses attention on 'RS   '.

Those who value their computer principally for number crunching may not be particularly excited with the prospect of dealing with strings and substrings. Nevertheless, there are some situations in which modest ability in substring maneuvers will prove mighty handy. The accompanying example may provide an inkling.

```
C
C EXAMPLE WITH SUBSTRINGS - COUNTING C'S
C
      CHARACTER*20 NAME
      INTEGER COUNT
      READ*, NAME
      COUNT = 0
      DO 3 K= 1,20
         IF (NAME(K:K) .EQ. 'C') THEN
            COUNT = COUNT + 1
         ENDIF
    3 CONTINUE
      PRINT*,' COUNT =', COUNT
      END
```

Here, following declaration of the variable NAME a free-format READ is performed. We may assume that somebody's name is read in. You remembered, no doubt, that

---

[2]   Following standard practice, single literal characters and strings in text are generally enclosed within open and close quote marks. For situations in which this would lead to incorrect Fortran, we follow correct Fortrran style and use close quote marks both before and after characters and strings. To assure successful treatment of CHARACTER data, etc., use only the single close quote mark before and after each constant.

the name is necessarily enclosed in single quote marks. Next the DO 3 loop takes over; as the value of K increases each iteration of the loop, successive characters, that is, successive one-character substrings in NAME, are compared to 'C'. Whenever a match is found the value stored on variable COUNT is incremented by one, so when the DO 3 loop completes, variable COUNT holds the count of Cs found in whatever was read into NAME.

2.7 Character Functions

The nature of type CHARACTER precludes doing anything corresponding direct-ly with arithmetic operations, but CHARACTER parts can be hooked together. The magic word for this is **concatenation.** Perhaps you have done this sort of thing with files, using an editor. The operation symbol this time is two slashes, or two division symbols if you prefer. With the variables declared and the values assigned in section 2.5, we could build '5PANTHERS' with NAME= KEY//TEAM. In this case any other attempt to concatenate with these variables cannot be accomodated.

Although ordinary computations can't be done with characters, they can be sen-sibly compared. The relational operators can be used to determine whether the con-tents of two character variables are equal, to identify the larger, or to compare a variable's contents to a constant. This paves the way for arranging things in alphabeti-cal order, etc. Additionally, there are two functions that deal with CHARACTER type. One, not surprisingly named CHAR, is a CHARACTER function that operates on an integer argument. A simple example of this is:

```
C ILLUSTRATION OF FUNCTION CHAR
C
      CHARACTER BB, CC
      BB = CHAR (54)
      CC = CHAR (55)
      PRINT*, BB, CC
      STOP
      END
```

The example shows variables BB and CC properly declared, then assigned the result of whatever CHAR does with the integers 54 and 55. After just a little coaxing, one Fortran yielded V and W as the results, whereas another Fortran came up with 6 and 7. Perhaps you are wondering why two creditable compilers would produce such starkly different results. The answer is that each Fortran has its own **collating sequence.** This is the sequence in which the characters are recognized by the com-piler. By now you know this is not standard across all Fortrans. Actually, only a couple of sequence characteristics are required of all Fortrans: B is larger than A, etc., and 5 is larger than 4, as the characters are represented internally.

All this probably comes as no great surprise. Without being aware of the details, most of us realize that the internal representation for all those letters and numerals is numeric in nature. Most of us would go along with the internal numeric repre-sentation for B being a tad larger than that for A. A hitch might develop when we tried to agree whether the smallest letter should be smaller or larger than the largest digit.

Evidently, agreement on this was no longer possible when the Fortran moguls convened to standardize their wares. So the collating sequence for your Fortran may have numerals first, then letters, then again it may not. That's where CHAR comes in. With this function at your disposal, you can probe around and establish your own—well, your Fortran's own—collating sequence. The complementary function ICHAR works the same, but the other way around. This is an integer function working on a CHARACTER argument. For example, following M= ICHAR('B'), one Fortran says 34, the other says 98, when instructed to print out M. Try out these functions soon.

2.8 Exercises 2-1

The capacity for comparing and manipulating individual characters and groups of characters provides a whole new dimension in which the fledgling programmer can operate. Confirm your grasp of the new data type by dealing with these exercises.

1. Explore the collating sequence of the system that serves you. Prepare a three sentence report setting forth your most important discoveries.

2. Assign a string of five different characters to a five character variable. Extend the program to print out the characters in reverse order. Next, print the five characters out in original order from left to right across the top and down the left side of a square and in reverse order along the bottom and down the right side.

3. Prepare a program that reads in strings of 40 lower case letters and prints out the same character strings but with capital letters.

4. Write a program to read in and encrypt a message consisting of strings of up to 40 characters. Use the collating sequence to assign numbers to each character in the message.

5. Construct a program that will identify the position of a given three-character substring embedded in strings of up to 40 random characters.

6. Prepare a sample of your own writing in a data file. Then run a program that reads in a letter and finds the number of times that letter appears in the example of your work.

7. Read in a string of up to 40 characters and delete all vowels and blank spaces. Print the result.

8. Write a program to read in three strings; call them MESSAGE, OLDSTRING, and NEWSTRING. Replace every occurrence of OLDSTRING in MESSAGE by NEWSTRING.

9. Develop a program to check for 'palindromes' (strings that have the same character sequence from left to right and right to left, as in *stats* or *mom*).

10. Using your knowledge of library functions and the collating sequence of your compiler, generate a list of random 6 character passwords for new computer accounts.

2.9 Subscripted Variables I

When humans begin getting serious about using Fortran, they usually need a surprising number of variable names. Most of us start selecting the names we use while under the influence of a whimsical preference for one or a few letters and numerals. A rather haphazard assortment of variable names develops. Frequently these are made up of fragments of girlfriends' or boyfriends' names and birth dates, etc. Before long the limits in this 'system' become evident, and serious programmers resolve to get organized in naming variables. A first effort in this direction frequently results in the selection of one or two alphabetical characters, together with one of a sequence of numbers. Other numbers in the sequence are combined with the letter to yield other names, for example, A1, A2, A3, etc. Most of us can keep track of our variable names more easily when they are arranged in such a sequence. In one sense, the business of subscripted variables can be regarded as an extension of the collective efforts of programmers to systematize the naming of variables. They do facilitate keeping track of a substantial number of variable names. Moreover as you will see, subscripted variables enable surprising economies within Fortran programs and truly phenomenal economies in programming input and output operations.

As it appears in the operation part of a Fortran instruction, a subscripted variable looks quite like a library function. A name is followed by a set of parens. The parens that belong to a subscripted variable contain something in integer mode. This can be either an integer variable or an integer constant. For example, AB(J55) and B6(3) are good, honest-sounding names for individual subscripted variables. Here the AB and the B6 indicate families of variables. The J55 and the 3 are the subscripts, identifying individual members of a family. Under ordinary circumstances, we would not expect any real constants nor any real variables within the parens belonging to a subscripted variable. If a real variable or constant were to appear within the parens here, the combination would probably be interpreted as a function (that is, similar to a library function).

Of course, the use of any program element as powerful and beneficial as a subscripted variable introduces some attendant problems. A programmer intending to use subscripted variables must tell the compiler in advance how many members are to be included in each subscripted variable 'family.'

Of the several ways to provide the needed information, the most basic is to use a DIMENSION statement. This statement appears first in the program and establishes the maximum number of subscripts that are to be recognized for each variable. For example:

```
DIMENSION A5(6),K3(4)
```

establishes 6 as the dimension for the subscripted variable A5 and 4 as the dimension for K3. In accordance with Fortran's default typing, the six A5s will each be regarded as real variables, whereas the four K3s will be integer.

In a Fortran program beginning with the example DIMENSION statement, the following individual variable names will be recognized:

A5(1) *Say "A-five of one"*   A5(5)   K3(2)
A5(2)   A5(6)   K3(3)
A5(3)   K3(1)   K3(4)
A5(4)

With all these different variable names beginning with A5 and K3, you must realize the hazard in naming another, unsubscripted variable in the same program as either A5 or K3. The compiler will appreciate your refraining from such double use of the same name for both a subscripted and an ordinary variable, etc. Also, resist the tendency to be vague when establishing the dimensions of subscripted variables. It is not acceptable to use DIMENSION A(K), no matter how sincere your intentions of revealing the value of the actual dimension later on. You can chisel a bit by setting dimensions larger than you need and then working within these limits. But each dimension in a DIMENSION statement must be an integer constant.

Within the program we could use variable A5(L), provided that a value were established for integer variable L, and further provided that this value were between 1 and 6. It should be evident that a value for L greater than 6 would be larger than the maximum specified for A5 in the DIMENSION statement. Although they are sometimes reluctant to mention it, compilers are usually offended by this sort of thing. Additionally, it seems advisable for beginners to avoid zero and negative subscripts, although provision can be made for using them. You can see that there are some ways to go astray when using subscripted variables.

Many people regard subscripted variables as equivalent to arrays. Singly subscripted variables are considered equivalent to single-dimension arrays, either row or column arrays. For instance, the variable K3 could be regarded as either the row array:

K3(1)   K3(2)   K3(3)   K3(4)

or the column array:

K3(1)
K3(2)
K3(3)
K3(4)

We can use individual array elements in the same way we use ordinary variables. They can be assigned practically any value, and then appear in the operation part of a subsequent statement. We can program reading into or printing out the value held by an individual subscripted variable. For example, the instruction:

```
.
READ*, K3(2)
.
```

will control reading of a single integer value into variable 'kay three of two.' The normal procedures for manipulation and exchange hold for subscripted variables. For example, the program segment:

```
    .
A5(3) = FLOAT(K3(2))
A5(4) = 6.0*A5(3) + A5(2)
    .
```

directs the present value of integer variable K3(2) to be converted to real and assigned to variable A5(3). Next, the value of A5(3) is to be multiplied by real 6. Then the product is to be augmented by the current value of variable A5(2) and assigned as the new value of variable A5(4).

In other circumstances, the family name for a subscripted variable can refer to the whole array. Suppose you wanted to read in values for 100 variables. Without a subscripted variable, the READ* instruction would be unduly lengthy, probably necessitating continuation on several program lines. One possible result is:

```
READ*, A1,A2,A3, . . . .A16,
1A17,A18,A19, . . . . .A32,A3
23,A34, . . . . . . .A48,A49,
 . . . . . . . . . . . . . .
 . . . . . . . . . . . . . .
6A96,A97,A98,A99,A100
    .
    .
```

The representation here shows a READ* instruction that is continued over several rows. The READ* begins in column 7 of the first row. The comma following the variable name A16 is represented as appearing in column 72 of the first row. The 1 in column 6 of the second row results in the row being considered a **continuation** of the READ* instruction. Each subsequent, nonzero numeral appearing in column 6 in a row causes the row to be considered a continuation of the preceding row.

If we were disposed to use a subscripted variable, the same amount of input could be accommodated as follows:

```
DIMENSION A(100)
READ* , A
```

In this segment the DIMENSION statement establishes 100 locations for variables with the name A. Having established this number of locations and having included A without a subscript in the READ* list, the computer gobbles up 100 data values. These will be deposited in turn in locations A(1), A(2), A(3), ... A(99), A(100). You can see what a great help subscripted variables can be for input and output of large amounts of information. Perhaps you can also appreciate that when we attempt to read into 100 individual locations in this way, at least 100 data values must be available. And if we program PRINT*, A, then the contents of all 100 locations will appear in the output.

Next for consideration is an example showing the utility of a subscripted variable within a program. Following the aforementioned reading of 100 data values, we could determine the largest of the values and its location in the sequence as follows:

```
C
C EXAMPLE TO IDENTIFY AND LOCATE THE MAXIMUM OF 100 VALUES
C
      DIMENSION A (100)
      READ*, A
      AMAX = 0.0
      DO 10 I = 1,100
         IF (AMAX .LT. A(I)) THEN
            AMAX = A(I)
            NPOS = I
         ENDIF
   10 CONTINUE
      PRINT*, AMAX, NPOS
      STOP
      END
```

The accompanying example illustrates several of the features recently introduced. First is the DIMENSION-READ* combination, which obtains 100 values and deposits them in the variables A. Think of these as strung out in a long line of positions, with the first value having been read into position one, the second into position two, and so on. Next, two variables are initialized to zero; real variable AMAX is set to 0.0 and integer variable NPOS is set to plain old zero without the decimal point. Thereafter, a DO loop is established, which takes the current value of AMAX and checks down the line of 100 values. As the loop index changes from 1 to 100, we look at different elements in the array, A(1), A(2), . . .A(100). If AMAX is ever found to be less than the particular A being considered, the value of AMAX is replaced by the value being examined. Immediately thereafter—well, for all practical purposes immediately—the contents of variable NPOS are replaced by the current value of I. Whenever the value of AMAX is not less than the contents of the A being considered, the THEN block is skipped. After the loop has been traversed 100 times, variable AMAX holds the largest of the 100 values read in, and NPOS holds the position in which the maximum value was found. The relatively small size of the array used in this example need not obscure the substantial help provided by the subscripted variable. If the extra effort needed to use subscripted variables doesn't yet seem worthwhile, try programming the example selection of a maximum using only ordinary variables.

As noted previously, the subscript, the thing appearing within the parens, which identifies an individual subscripted variable, can be either an integer constant or an integer variable for which a value has been established. The utility of subscripted variables is considerably enhanced by the option of using an integer expression in place of a single variable or constant as a subscript. For example, assuming suitable dimensions were established for variable X, then either X(N+1) or X(3*N+4) would illustrate valid subscript forms. Of course, the total value of the subscript is restricted to the range from one up to the maximum established by the related DIMENSION.

Although the recommendation here, especially for beginners, is to dimension arrays with integers running from one up to the size needed, 1977 Fortran enables some additional detail in establishing dimensions. We can use integers different from one to designate the first element in the array. For example, if data related to college students were being accumulated in an array the following might serve:

```
DIMENSION IAGE(16:30)
```

This establishes a 15-element array IAGE, but with the element designations running from 16 to 30 instead of from 1 to 15. When specified in this form the element designation is the same as the age of the student group from which the data is obtained; the first element, IAGE(16) holds data for 16-year-old students, etc. This option for establishing dimensions can be extended to include negative numbers and zero as valid subscripts.

When using subscripted variables, one isn't necessarily constrained to follow Fortran's convention for naming real and integer variables. The option of declaring a variable to be of the type desired can be incorporated with the dimensioning and reserving of space which otherwise is done by DIMENSION. For example, the declaration statements:

```
REAL MAD(500)
INTEGER ALFRED(10)
```

serve to establish both MAD and ALFRED as subscripted variables with space reserved as indicated. These declaration statements both establish the type and designate maximum subscript value for the specified variables. Evidently, in the ensuing program each MAD is to be regarded as a real variable, and each ALFRED as an integer variable.

Don't overlook the opportunity to use subscripted variables, or arrays, that are declared to be of type CHARACTER. These are similar to character strings although the symbols used to represent them are different. Some purposes are served as well by either a 100-character string or a 100-element character array. As you will see shortly, these can be used to produce some elementary graphic output. But remember the one-character limit; unless you declare otherwise, each location in a character array will accommodate only one character. Two Fortrans at hand will accept a DIMENSION statement with a separate CHARACTER declaration; these can be in either order as long as both appear in the program before any executable statement. The combination of the declaration together with the dimension, along the lines of the preceding paragraph, is recommended here. The declaration:

```
CHARACTER TUB(10)
```

establishes the data type of the variable, and instructs the compiler to reserve ten locations, each able to accommodate a single character. If you wanted each location in the array to be able to hold three characters, then of course you would use:

```
CHARACTER*3 TUX(10)
```

The advantage provided by arrays for processing substantial amounts of character input is limited when one is using free-format reading. This is so because of the requirement for each character or string read in being enclosed in the single quote marks. Accordingly the data line satisfying the READ*, TUB instruction would appear 'z' 'y' 'x', etc. and the line serving READ*, TUX could be 'abc' 'def' 'ghi', etc. Chances are that you will appreciate formatted reading, especially if you have need to read in lots of character data.

2.10 Looping Operations II

Participants who aspire to any but the most elementary level of programming skill will perforce become experienced loopers. A second level of related experience is indicated in the sections that follow. Items to be considered are loops within loops and special loops for input to and output from singly subscripted variables. Some attention is also devoted to loops for which simply counting the number of iterations may not yield the most desirable means of control. As will become evident, these program elements involve looping, in which control depends on some condition.

2.11 Nested DO Loops

Soon after learning about DO loops, most programmers ask about having one DO inside another DO. These are called nested DOs, and they serve well, provided the inner DO does not stick out through the bottom of the outer DO. Example?

```
C
C EXAMPLE SKELETON NESTED DO LOOPS
C
      DO 20 L = 1  ,10
         .
      DO 10 M = 1,5
         .
         .
10    CONTINUE
20 CONTINUE
      .
```

This program fragment presents a nested pair of DO loops. The outer, DO 20 loop is to be repeated 10 times. Each time, all instructions within its range are executed. As you can see, the inner DO 10 loop is within the range of the outer loop, so each time the outer loop is called into action, the inner loop is to be executed five times. The example indicates two worthwhile features. The first is provision of a separate CONTINUE for each DO, with each CONTINUE in line below its own DO. The second is the uniform indentation of all statements within the range of each DO. As noted previously, these features are not essential for proper functioning of your program, but they help human interpretation considerably.

A second example provides more details regarding the ways nested DOs work together. As you will see, the program makes use of a character array, using it several times to produce bar graphs. These graphs are one way of representing numerical values in graphic form. Although the programming skills encountered thus far don't enable very detailed graphics, there are times when some simple graphics can provide a boost to communication. In the present example the action begins by printing out a row of dots to appear as the top part of the border around the bar graphs. Next a value is read into integer variable NUM. This value is to establish the number of bar graphs to be produced. Variable NUM is used as the upper limit for LL, the control variable for the DO 10 loop. Just inside the DO 10 loop, the DO 8 loop swings into action and, as we say in the jargon of the trade, clears the character array BAR to blanks. Here the 50 iterations of the DO 8 loop assign alphanumeric blanks to each of the 50 elements in BAR. Keep in mind that the blank is a legitimate character, and note that there is a blank between the quote marks there in the single statement within the DO 8 loop.

```
C
C PROGRAM TO READ IN A SCORE THEN PRODUCE A BAR GRAPH
C TO REPRESENT THE SCORE FOR EACH OF NUM STUDENTS
C
      CHARACTER BAR(50)
      PRINT*,' .................................................... '
      READ*, NUM
      DO 10 LL = 1,NUM
         DO 8 IC = 1,50
            BAR(IC) = ' '
8        CONTINUE
         READ *, SCORE
         IX = INT(SCORE/100.0 * 50.0)
         DO 9 IC = 1,IX
            BAR(IC) = '#'
9        CONTINUE
         PRINT*,' .'
         PRINT*,' .',BAR,'                                       .'
      10 CONTINUE
      PRINT*,' .................................................... '
      END
```

Next a real value is read into variable SCORE; we may surmise all values here will range up to a maximum of 100.0. The next instruction reduces the score to a scale of 50.0, so it can be represented by the number of elements in BAR. The value computed and assigned to variable IX will be in the range from 0 to 50, in proportion to the student's score. Now the DO 9 loop goes to work and fills in the double-cross characters in all locations in BAR, up to the one numbered IX. The blanks previously assigned to the other BAR elements remain in place. The first of the two contiguous PRINT* instructions provides spacing between the individual bar graphs and the dots are for the side borders. The statement that prints BAR includes the border-forming dots as well as the variable BAR. Inasmuch as BAR appears without subscript, the contents of all 50 locations will be printed out. After the DO 10 loop completes the NUMth time, the row of dots forming the bottom border is printed and the program terminates. In this example, to produce bar graphs for eight students the DO 10 loop will be executed eight times. For each iteration of the DO 10 loop, the DO 8 loop is executed 50 times and the DO 9 loop will be executed a number of times proportionate to the score represented. A typical output from a bar graph program representing eight scores is shown here.

```
. . . . . . . . . . . . . . . . . . . . . . . . . . . . . . . . . . . . . . . . . . . . . . . . . . . .
.                                                                         .
. #####################                                                   .
.                                                                         .
. ######                                                                  .
.                                                                         .
. #############################################                          .
.                                                                         .
. ###############                                                         .
.                                                                         .
. ####                                                                    .
.                                                                         .
. #####################################################                  .
.                                                                         .
. ##########################################                             .
.                                                                         .
. ########################################################               .
.                                                                         .
. . . . . . . . . . . . . . . . . . . . . . . . . . . . . . . . . . . . . . . . . . . . . . . . . . . .
```

2.12 Implied DO Loops

Sometimes the regular DO can be awkward to use. For instance, if a READ* instruction is included within the range of a regular DO, then each time the loop is executed at least one new line of data will be needed. All this can be rather inconvenient, for instance, if we wanted to read a bunch of values into a subscripted variable. Any attempt to thus read all or even a group of data values from the same line in the data file leads to disappointment. This is because each time control transfers to the READ*, a new data row must be provided. We can deal with this situation handily with an **implied** DO.

The implied DO is sort of a stripped down version of a regular DO. This one is especially serviceable when we are concerned with input to or output from a subscripted variable. For example:

```
READ*, (A(K),K = 1,100)
```

will control the input of values into 100 locations of variable A. Of course, a suitable DIMENSION or declaration statement would necessarily be present earlier in the program.

Perhaps the attentive reader is wondering how this is any improvement over:

```
DIMENSION A(100)
READ*, A
```

Well, there may not be any. However, variable A could have been dimensioned for more than 100, but with values to be read only into the first 100 locations in the array. We might also want to use an implied DO as follows:

```
READ 78, (A(K),K = 1,100,5)
```

Here the third number, the 5 following the control variable, specifies the amount by which the variable is to be incremented at each iteration. This incrementing can be done the same way with a regular DO. In either instance take care to observe that the locations receiving values would be A(1), A(6), A(11), etc. Also, when using an implied DO, note that there is a comma in there just ahead of the control variable. It's these little things that keep programmers on their toes.

2.13 Sorting Example

Let's hope that along about now you are ready for a comprehensive example that shows some of the recently-considered Fortran elements at work. The accompanying example has been prepared to do just that, with some emphasis on singly subscripted variables, or arrays. The program listing has been augmented with a column of line numbers on the left; it should be clear that these are not part of the program, their purpose is to facilitate text reference to specific lines. As you can see, a block of comments occupies the first 20 lines of the listing; things begin to happen in line 21.

```
 1 C
 2 C THIS EXAMPLE PROGRAM FILLS A 100-ELEMENT SUBSCRIPTED VARIABLE
 3 C WITH LETTERS SELECTED AT RANDOM. THE LETTERS ARE SORTED INTO
 4 C ALPHABETICAL ORDER. NEXT THE COUNTS ARE ESTABLISHED FOR EACH
 5 C LETTER AND STORED IN A 26-ELEMENT INTEGER ARRAY. THE INTEGER
 6 C ARRAY IS SEARCHED TO DETERMINE THE LETTER HAVING THE GREATEST
 7 C COUNT. THE CONTENTS OF THE INTEGER ARRAY ARE PRINTED IN TWO
 8 C COLUMNS, TOGETHER WITH THE CORRESPONDING LETTERS. FINALLY,
 9 C THE MOST FREQUENTLY OCCURRING LETTER IS PRINTED WITH ITS COUNT.
10 C
11 C THE EXAMPLE ILLUSTRATES USE OF THE FOLLOWING.
12 C
13 C 1. SINGLY SUBSCRIPTED INTEGER AND CHARACTER ARRAYS
14 C 2. LIBRARY FUNCTION RANF TO OBTAIN RANDOM NUMBERS
15 C 3. LIBRARY FUNCTION INT TO CONVERT REAL TO INTEGER
16 C 4. FUNCTIONS CHAR AND ICHAR FOR CHARACTERS AND COUNTS
17 C 5. NESTED DO LOOPS
18 C 6. IMPLIED DO LOOPS
19 C 7. INTEGER EXPRESSIONS AS SUBSCRIPTS
20 C
21       CHARACTER HAT(100),TEMP,C1,C2,C3
22       INTEGER KOUNT(26)
23 C
24 C GET THE LETTERS AND PUT THEM IN HAT
25 C
26       DO 10 IR = 1,100
27          ANUM = RANF(0.0)
28          NNUM = INT(33.0+26.0*ANUM)
29          HAT(IR) = CHAR(NNUM)
30 10    CONTINUE
31 C
32 C PRINT OUT THE RANDOM LETTERS
33 C
34       PRINT*, HAT
```

```
35 C
36 C USE NESTED DO'S TO DO THE SORTING
37 C
38       DO 30 IX = 1,99
39          DO 20 J = 1,99
40             IF(HAT(J) .GT. HAT(J+1)) THEN
41                TEMP = HAT(J)
42                HAT(J) = HAT(J+1)
43                HAT(J+1) = TEMP
44             ENDIF
45 20       CONTINUE
46 30    CONTINUE
47 C
48 C PRINT OUT THE SORTED LETTERS
49 C
50       PRINT*,(HAT(IX), IX=1,50)
51       PRINT*,(HAT(IY), IY=51,100)
52 C
53 C CLEAR ARRAY KOUNT TO ZEROS
54 C
55       DO 40 IZ = 1,26
56 40    KOUNT(IZ) = 0
57 C
58 C ESTABLISH THE COUNTS FOR EACH LETTER
59 C THEN SEARCH KOUNT FOR THE MAXIMUM
60 C
61       DO 50 IX = 1,100
62          KK = ICHAR(HAT(IX)) - 32
63          KOUNT(KK) = KOUNT(KK) + 1
64 50    CONTINUE
65       MAX = 0
66       DO 60 IX = 1,26
67          IF(MAX .LT. KOUNT(IX)) THEN
68             MAX = KOUNT(IX)
69             IDENT = IX + 32
70          ENDIF
71 60    CONTINUE
72 C
73 C PRINT OUT LETTERS AND COUNTS, THEN THE HI-COUNT LETTER
74 C
75       DO 70 IR = 1,13
76          IP = IR + 13
77          C1 = CHAR(IR+32)
78          C2 = CHAR(IP+32)
79          PRINT*, C1,KOUNT(IR), C2,KOUNT(IP)
80 70    CONTINUE
81       C3 = CHAR(IDENT)
82       PRINT*, C3, MAX
83       END
```

In line 21, variable HAT is declared as a CHARACTER variable, dimensioned 100. Inasmuch as no size designation is present, each location in HAT, as well as each of the other variables declared with it, is capable of holding only one character. The declaration in line 22 establishes KOUNT as subscripted with dimension of 26. Inasmuch as the default data type for a variable named KOUNT is integer, the provision for subscripting could have been done as well with a DIMENSION statement.

The DO 10 loop, beginning on line 26, uses the library function RANF. When supplied with 0.0 as argument, the function returns a decimal fraction between 0.0 and 1.0. Some refer to the argument 0.0 as the seed for the random number generator; the seed gets the function going. Seeding the function in this way may seem strange, but it works. Each time through the DO 10 loop a new random number is assigned to variable ANUM. Inasmuch as ANUM can have a value anywhere between 0.0 and 1.0, 26.0*ANUM can have any value between 0.0 and 26.0, and the operation within the parens in line 28 will yield a real number from 33.0 to 59.0. But the library function INT changes the value to an integer, so any decimal fraction part is lost in the transformation. The integer is assigned to variable NNUM, which next serves as the argument for the function CHAR. Evidently, in the collating sequence in service here, CHAR(33) is 'A', etc. Of course, the collating sequence serving you will very likely be different, so if you get curious about all this you will just have to make the necessary adjustments and run the example program. During each iteration of the DO 10 loop, an integer value is assigned to NNUM and then supplied to CHAR. CHAR returns a letter and it is assigned to the next location in array HAT. When the DO 10 loop has terminated, each location in HAT will hold one letter. The PRINT* in line 34 will print out the contents of the whole array.

Sorting HAT's contents is done in the nest of DO loops beginning on line 38. To be sure of ordering 100 items, the sequence of 99 comparisons must be made 99 times. The inner DO 20 loop controls the 99 comparisons; the outer DO 30 loop assures that the comparisons will all be done 99 times. All these comparisons are needed to provide for the worst possible case, for instance when the character 'A' would happen to be in HAT(100) before the sorting begins.

The first time the inner loop is entered, the content of HAT(1) is compared with that of HAT(2). The next iteration of the inner loop compares the contents of HAT(2) and HAT(3), etc. Whenever the contents of adjacent array elements are found to be out of the desired order, the contents are interchanged in the block IF beginning on line 40. For example, if HAT(7) is found to hold a 'larger' letter than HAT(8) holds, then the contents of the two array elements are switched. After the inner loop has done its thing 99 times, control transfers from the 20 CONTINUE to the 30 CONTINUE and then back to the DO 30. Now the inner loop is entered again, and the 99 comparisons are repeated. As you can see, this is not an especially efficient way of performing the sorting. Probably you are already thinking of a better way.

Lines 50 and 51 illustrate the use of implied DOs; each one prints out half of the HAT array after it has been sorted. Next the DO 40 loop clears the KOUNT array; the value zero is assigned to each of the 26 array elements. If you don't see much purpose in this, look ahead to line 63; note KOUNT(KK) in the operation part of the statement.

If a value had not been established for each location in KOUNT, then there would be a rumble about an undefined variable. Inasmuch as the locations in KOUNT are used to accumulate counts, we need to set each location to zero before counting begins. Observe, there is no CONTINUE at the bottom of the DO 40 loop. The fact is, you can use practically any executable instruction to complete the loop in place of the CONTINUE. Lots of programmers use the form shown here when there is only one instruction in the loop. This also saves a line when we are trying to get lots of lines printed on a page. One thing further, the example displays considerable reluctance to use the same integer variable to control successive loops, for instance IX and IY are used to control the implied DOs, then variable IZ is used to control the DO 40 loop. In general these changes are not necessary. After a loop completes, the same control variable can be used for the next loop. Of course when the loops are nested, as shown in lines 38 to 46, one must use a different control variable to run the inner loop.

The DO 50 loop obtains, in turn, the contents of each element of variable HAT. Suppose, for example, HAT(1) is 'B'; evidently ICHAR will return the integer 34, at least with the collating sequence represented here. But the count of Bs is to be kept in KOUNT(2), that's why the 32 is subtracted there in line 62. The function ICHAR will provide an integer in the range 33 to 59, depending on the position of a letter in the collating sequence. Variable KK will get a value in the range 1 to 26, each value effectively pointing to an element in array KOUNT. In the present instance the value of KK is 2, so the action represented in line 63 augments the contents of KOUNT(2) by one. After the DO 50 loop has completed, each location in KOUNT will hold the count for the corresponding letter.

Next, the search for a maximum is to be made in subscripted variable KOUNT. To prepare for the search, variable MAX is initialized to zero and then the DO 60 loop is entered. We may be reasonably confident that the first time through the loop the contents of KOUNT(1) will be greater than zero, so whatever is in KOUNT(1) is assigned to MAX. This sort of action is repeated each iteration of the loop. Whenever a location in KOUNT is found to hold a value greater than that in MAX, then MAX gets a new value and the instruction in line 69 assigns a new value to IDENT. The value assigned is the current loop index plus 32. The 32 is needed because the second element in KOUNT, holding the count of the Bs, corresponds to the thirty-fourth location in the collating sequence. When the DO 60 loop has completed, MAX will hold the count of the most frequent letter, and IDENT will refer to the position of the letter in the collating sequence.

The DO 70 loop directs printing 13 rows of four columns. The first column holds characters (letters) in alphabetical order from top to bottom. The second column holds the counts for the letters appearing in the first column. The third and fourth columns hold similar information, but for the second half of the alphabet. Finally, CHAR(IDENT) is assigned to variable C3, and this is printed out together with the value of MAX. Check through the operations in this example a time or two. Make sure you grasp the way the variable KOUNT is linked to the collating sequence. Review the seven numbered items at the beginning of the program, and practice identifying the points in the program to which each item refers.

2.14 Exercises 2-2

A recent example has featured a singly subscripted variable, or one-dimension array if you prefer, holding characters. Of course, integer and real arrays are equally serviceable and of comparable advantage when large amounts of information are to be processed. In your efforts with the exercises that follow, make sure you practice with arrays of all three data types. In all instances refrain from exceeding the dimensions you have established. And remember that clearing character arrays to blanks, and real and integer arrays to zeros is often worthwhile, and sometimes essential.

1. Prepare a program that reads in groups of 20 integers. If the sum of the integers is an even number, print out the first, then the third, then the fifth, etc. of the numbers. If the sum of the integers read in is an even number, print out the second, then the fourth, etc.

2. Run a program that reads in a group of real numbers then computes their mean and the standard deviation. Make sure your program can handle different size groups of up to 100 real values. Identify the real number having the smallest difference from the mean, print out the number and its position in the list as read in; print only the first if there are duplicates. Check your value for standard deviation with an alternative computation.

3. Sort a list of integers from highest to lowest value using a bubble sort as shown in example 2.13. Compute the median and mode of these data. Confirm your program's ability to deal with lists of different sizes.

4. Devise a program to read in two columns of integers. Sort each in ascending order then merge the two columns into a third column also in ascending order.

5. Given two lists of integers, write a program to find the first integer common to both lists.

6. The Fibonacci sequence is given as 1,1,2,3,5,8,13,21, . . . , where the the first two terms are 1 and all other terms are the sum of the two preceding terms. Compute the first 100 terms of the Fibonnaci sequence and print them in reverse order.

7. Read in 20 positive integers and identify all possible pairings of those integers that total between 50 and 75.

8. Write a program to determine the number of positive integer coordinates that lie in the circle $X**2 + Y**2 = 50$. How would you modify the program to find all (positive and negative) integer coordinates?

9. Run a program that fills a character array with 100 letters of the alphabet selected at random. Search the array and count the instances in which any letter is paired with itself and for instances of three of the same letter appearing in sequence. Repeat the operation 100 times and compare the

counts obtained with values you would expect based on your knowledge of the alphabet and of random selection.

10. Run a program using one singly subscripted character variable to plot two transcendental functions. For example plot $X_1 = 2SIN(Y)$ and $X_2 = COS(2Y)$ together.

2.15 WHILE Loops

Those stalwarts foolhardy enough to attempt writing instructions for using Fortran soon find they are tracking a moving target. Fortran just isn't like it used to be, and it keeps changing, seemingly all the time. Well, it isn't quite that bad, but the current topic presents a good example. At the present writing, WHILE loops are not included in standard Fortran. Perhaps you can guess why when you are told that some Fortrans respond to 'WHILE-DO' whereas others insist on 'DO-WHILE.' Which one of these will work for you? You may just have to try each to make sure. But remember, neither has been adopted as an official feature, so quite possibly neither one is 'up on your system,' as we say, ready to serve you. If such grim fate is your lot, check the next section, and do the best you can.

In contrast to the regular DO, which is a **counter controlled** loop, the WHILE is a **condition controlled** loop. This provides an advantage over counter control when the programmer doesn't have advanced knowledge of the number of times a loop must be repeated to achieve a desired result.

The accompanying example includes a WHILE loop that produces the square root of a number that is read in. Computation of the root is done in three steps. First, the number to be rooted is divided by an arbitrary estimated root. Next, the estimate and the quotient are added and then divided by two to yield the average of the two values. If all goes well, the average will be closer to the desired root than was the estimate. Then the difference between the original estimate and the newly computed average is determined; this is the value that will terminate the loop. The looping continues until the value drops below a specified limit. The next instruction in the loop assigns the computed average to the variable ESTIM, in preparation for repeating the loop (see next page for program).

The virtue of the WHILE is evident here; looping will be continued only until the desired precision is obtained. The ENDWHILE statement establishes the bottom of the loop, and the statement following ENDWHILE will be executed only when the WHILE condition becomes false. For any original estimate, the number of loop iterations needed will be different for different numbers read in. The WHILE adapts to this and shuts off looping just after the desired control value is obtained. For protection against foul-up, a counter is established to prevent a runaway loop. Note, too, some value must be established for DIFF before the loop is entered. This necessity is characteristic of the WHILE.

```
C
C WHILE LOOP USED IN COMPUTING SQUARE ROOTS
C
      READ*, ANUM
      IF(ANUM .LT. 0.0) STOP
      ESTIM = 100.0
      DIFF = 1.0
      LIMIT = 0
      WHILE (DIFF .GT. 1.0E-10) DO
         STEP1 = ANUM/ESTIM
         STEP2 = STEP1 + ESTIM
         STEP3 = STEP2/2.0
         DIFF = ABS(ESTIM-STEP3)
         ESTIM = STEP3
         LIMIT = LIMIT + 1
            IF (LIMIT .GT. 20) THEN
               PRINT*, LIMIT, ANUM, ESTIM
               STOP
            ENDIF
      ENDWHILE
      PRINT*, ANUM, STEP3
      END
```

2.16 Fortran's GO TO

Those who consider the WHILE to be a programming feature that hasn't quite (at least officially) arrived may regard the GO TO as a feature that has remained too long. Indeed, many programmers feel strongly that GO TOs should be stricken from any approved list of program instructions. But if no other means for conditional control of looping is available, an occasional GO TO may forestall considerable torment. We used to say that, in conjunction with an IF, the GO TO provides conditional transfer of control. This is about the same as conditional execution, but the other way around. The combination IF-GO TO enables getting out of a counter-controlled loop before the counter has run its full course. Whereas the WHILE-DO does just what it says, the present combination fulfills the complementary function: AS SOON AS-QUIT. You will see the combination at work in the next example. The example is similar to the last one, but with the loop control replaced.

```
C
C DO LOOP WITH CONDITIONAL EXIT USED TO
C COMPUTE SQUARE ROOTS
C
      READ*, ANUM
      IF(ANUM .LT. 0.0) STOP
      ESTIM = 100.0
      DIFF = 1.0
      DO 60 M = 1,20
         IF(DIFF .LT. 1.0E-10) GO TO 65
         STEP1 = A1UM/ESTIM
         STEP2 = STEP1 + ESTIM
         STEP3 = STEP2/2.0
         DIFF = ABS(ESTIM-STEP3)
         ESTIM = STEP3
   60 CONTINUE
   65 CONTINUE
      PRINT*, ANUM, STEP3
      END
```

As you can see in this example, the essential loop control is provided by the DO. Inasmuch as the loop is limited to 20 trips, there is no need to protect against a runaway. If the result becomes acceptable before the looping is complete, the IF-GO TO transfers control to statement 65 outside the loop. Whether to use this one or the last method may well depend on what is available. If a WHILE is available, use it. If one isn't, one probably will be before long. Until then you may have to struggle along with the older control, but resolve to be sparing in your use of Fortran's GO TO.

2.17 Formatted Output

Free-format, or list-directed, output is a great convenience for beginning programmers. It enables beginners and others for whom rudimentary output serves adequately to program without concern for details that can get a bit sticky. Nevertheless the programming needs of all but the most casual users soon prompt consideration of ways to put the output where the user wants it, instead of where free-format dictates. The cause for present concern is evident in the output from one of the programming exercises. As produced by one system, the first five rows of output appear as follows:

```
1.000000000000    1.000000000000    1.000000000000
2.000000000000    4.000000000000    8.000000000000
3.000000000000    9.000000000000    27.00000000000
4.000000000000    16.00000000000    64.00000000000
5.000000000000    25.00000000000    125.0000000000
```

Output from the same program run on another system appears next:

```
1.000000000000    1.000000000000    1.000000000000
2.000000000000    4.000000000000    8.000000000000
3.000000000000    9.000000000000    .2700000000000E+02
4.000000000000    .1600000000000E+02    .6400000000000E+02
5.000000000000    .2500000000000E+02    .1250000000000E+03
```

Three features in particular may be objectionable. In the first field of both examples of output, where we really want just the whole numbers from 1 to 10, the numbers seem unduly burdened with all those zeros. When using free-format there is no way for the programmer to eliminate the zeros and get plain old 1., 2., 3., etc. Next, when the value represented changes to 10 and larger, the position of the decimal point is seen to shift to the right in the first example. This can make scanning of an output column wearisome, sometimes even hazardous. In the second output example, the position of the point shifts the other way and the format changes. It could be that the programmer doesn't want the output in exponential form, but there is no way to prevent it. Finally, when using free-format, the number of output columns that can appear on either a terminal screen or an output page is unduly limited. You may have encountered this condition in one of the exercises. If you did not sense the problem (did you do the exercise?) and are content with the output provided by free-format, then by all means continue using it. But if you agree that free-format isn't altogether free, then give some consideration to output formatting.

Several types of format are available. The first to be considered is referred to as F-type. This type accommodates values from real variables. As it appears in the program, the FORMAT is linked to its PRINT by means of a statement number. Note that the asterisk is dropped from the PRINT* instruction when providing for formatted output. The number appears in place of the asterisk in the PRINT and again in columns 1-5 in the line containing the FORMAT. Any number from 1 to 99999 can be used for linking the PRINT and the FORMAT. If the number 555 were chosen, the combination of statements would shape up as follows:

```
      PRINT 555, A, B, C
  555 FORMAT( F )
```

You may suspect that something beside the letter F goes there within the parens in the FORMAT statement. But before worrying about that, pause long enough to appreciate the way the two statements are linked together by the number 555. It appears right after the PRINT and also as the statement number of the FORMAT. The numbered FORMAT statement doesn't have to be next after the PRINT. FORMAT statements can appear anywhere in the program. Given the number in the PRINT instruction, transfer is made to the FORMAT and the necessary information is obtained and brought back to the PRINT. Two related points merit consideration here. First, only one statement in a program can have 555 as its statement number; the same holds for any other number. Second, any practical number of PRINT statements can use the same FORMAT. Lots of discriminating programmers put all the FORMATs just before the END of a program. This facilitates finding them readily, to see if an existing FORMAT can serve a second PRINT and to ensure that there is no double use of a statement number.

As you have no doubt guessed by now, the FORMAT statement is to provide information for the PRINT. The information serves to locate the output values along each row as it is printed or as it appears at the terminal. This is done by specifying the width of the field in which each value is to appear and the location of the decimal point within each field. The field width is indicated by the number that appears within the parens following the F. If, for example, the number is 10.3, then the F-type field is to be ten columns wide. As the output value appears, there will be a decimal point in the field. The point will be positioned so that three digits appear to its right; that's what the 3 in the F10.3 provides. With this field specification the position of the decimal point will not shift as the output values change.

The example F 10.3 field can be repeated in the FORMAT statement, separating successive field specifications (specs) with commas. The same effect can be obtained by placing an appropriate number ahead of the F there within the parens in the FORMAT. The combination (3F10.3) would provide the same control as (F10.3,F10.3,F10.3). Of course, different field widths and decimal positions can be included in one FORMAT. If the combination:

```
PRINT 22, A, B, C
22 FORMAT(1X,F4.0,2F8.1)
```

were used in the program producing the last example output, the first row of output would appear as follows:

```
          1         2         3
12345678901234567890123456789 0
   1.      1.0     1.0
```

Quite so, the first two rows of numbers would not appear with the output. These serve as column indicators; they are shown here to help identify the columns in which the output appears. The four-column field that accommodates A's value does not begin in the first output column because the 1X directs skipping this column. This moves all output values over one column. Variable A's value appears in columns 2 through 5; nothing appears to the right of the first decimal point because the field spec is 4.0. B's value appears in a field that extends from column 6 to column 13. Since the specification for the second field is 8.1, one zero appears on the right of the decimal point.

As noted, the 1X first within the parens moves everything in the row of output over one column. This ensures that anything that might be directed to column 1 will be moved over into the second column. By thus preventing anything from ever appearing in the first column, the 1X provides protection against an undesirable signal being sent when output is routed to a line printer. Habitual use of the 1X first within the parens of output FORMATs is recommended. Well, yes, if you wanted all the values in the row shifted over ten spaces, then use 10X; but unless you have reason to do otherwise, use at least the 1X.

If the number of fields specified in a FORMAT is less than the number of variables to be accommodated, there will be extra rows of output. If (20X,F8.3) had been used in a FORMAT in the current example series, the output would appear similar to that shown here.

```
123456789012345678901234567890123456789O
                    1.000
                    1.000
                    1.000
                    2.000
                    4.000
                    8.000
```

Inasmuch as only one field is provided for output, each individual value fills all the field(s) available on a row. Whenever the computer uses all the available fields in a FORMAT yet still has more variables to print out, it simply uses the same FORMAT on a new row. If your Fortran implementation is one that doesn't recognize the PRINT instruction, then the same formatting can be obtained with a WRITE instruction. The statement:

```
WRITE(*,22) A, B, C
```

would serve in place of the PRINT 22 in the current example.

With formatted output many more output columns are possible than with free-format, however there are a couple of hazards. First, an individual field can be too narrow to accommodate the value intended. The value 125.5, for example, just won't fit in an F6.3 field. The value is said to **overflow** the field. Remember to count the output column required by the decimal point! Suspect overflow if unwanted asterisks appear where numbers should be in the output. **Underflow** is also possible. If the field specification is F6.2 and the value is 0.0035, the significant part of the the output will effectively slip through the cracks in the floor.

2.18 Exponential Form and E FORMAT

An earlier example of output shows a change in FORMAT type when the value printed changes from 9.0 to 10.0, for example. The output of 10.0 as 0.10000E 02, or 0.10000E+02, is as it would appear when printed out under E-type FORMAT. The E+02 indicates the need to multiply something by 10.0*10.0, as in scientific notation. This feature enables accommodating very large or very small values without overflow or underflow. Thus E-type is recommended when providing for output of those out-sized values. Minor differences exist among compilers in their processing of E-type FORMAT. If you must locate and represent output exactly, some experimentation with your system may be essential. The example to follow illustrates several points regarding E-and F-types. Note first the example's use of exponential form for the constants assigned to variables C and D. This form is generally acceptable for constants in Fortran expressions. Variable A could as well have been assigned the value 1.23456E+02, etc.

The present example program yields output in 15-column fields, although the field specification used first is (1X, F14.6). Be sure to note the way a field combination is repeated. The 4(1X,F14.6) repeats the field combination within the parens four times, which is much easier than using (1X, F14.6, 1X, F14.6, 1X, F14.6, 1X, F14.6). The spacing of the output is practically the same as it would have been with 4F15.6, except for the location of the asterisk in the first output row. If 4F15.6 had been used, the asterisk would appear right next to the six zeros, at least on one implementation of Fortran. Next, observe each of the field specifications carefully. Check the configuration of the output values and confirm the result of using the .6 in both E and F fields. The result is, of course, the presence of six output columns to the right of the decimal point, at least at first. Pay attention to the underflow of variable C's value in the first row of output and to the asterisk showing there was overflow because the F14.6 field could not accommodate the value of variable D. You can see the FORMAT was changed from F-type to E-type when D was printed the first time. Your compiler may or may not make such changes; some will simply print a bunch of asterisks instead of attempting to print a value in a field that is too small.

```
C EXAMPLE PROGRAM ILLUSTRATING EXPONENTIAL FORM OF CONSTANTS
C AND OUTPUT WITH BOTH E- AND F-TYPE FORMAT
C
      A = 123.456
      B = 0.00078912
C
C VARIABLES C AND D ARE ASSIGNED EXPONENTIAL-FORM CONSTANTS
C
      C = 9.876E-13
      D = 5.432E 29
      PRINT 101, A, B, C, D
      PRINT 102, A, B, C, D
      PRINT 103, A, B, C, D
      PRINT 104, A, B, C, D
C
C NOTE THE REPEATED FIELD COMBINATION IN 101
C
  101 FORMAT (1X,4(1X,F14.6))
  102 FORMAT (1X,4E15.6)
  103 FORMAT (1X,4(2PE15.6))
  104 FORMAT (1X,4(4PE15.6))
      STOP
      END
```

The output resulting from running the example is as follows:

```
          1         2         3         4         5         6
12345678901234567890123456789012345678901234567890123456789012345

    123.456000        .000789        .000000 * .5432000E+30
    .123456E+03    .789120E-03    .987600E-12    .543200E+30
    12.34560E+01   78.91200E-05   98.76000E-14   54.32000E+28
    1234.56E-01    7891.2E-07     9876.0E-16     5432.0E+26
```

A final point of potential interest is the use of scale factors in the program statements numbered 103 and 104. The 2P moves two digits over on the left side of the decimal point, and the 4P moves four, as they appear in the output. Let's hope you can fathom the result of using 1P or 3P with F fields.

A minor hazard relates to the capacity of the output device to be used. If more than 80 columns are to appear on a terminal screen, the output may 'wrap around,' appearing to continue on the next screen line. This isn't too bad, although confident interpretation of the output may present problems. When output is routed to a line printer, the number of output columns is limited to about 130. This may vary depending on the printer, but there is no wrap around. So if an output FORMAT exceeds the printer's column limit, a crash becomes likely.

2.19 Labeling Formatted Output

In addition to controlling the spacing of output, FORMAT facilitates labeling the output. Desired labels are included within single quote marks either with or in place of the field specs. For example, to provide headings for three columns of figures, each ten columns wide, try:

```
    PRINT 202
202 FORMAT (2X,'COLUMN 1' ,2X,'COLUMN 2' ,2X,
    1'COLUMN 3' ,//)
```

You may well wonder about a couple of items that were slipped into this example. These will be attended to soon. But first observe that if only labels are wanted, there is no variable list in the PRINT, just the statement number of the FORMAT holding the labels. The two statements, the PRINT and the FORMAT, don't have to appear together in the program. If the FORMAT is, say, together with other FORMATs near the end of the program, the link provided by the statement number will work just as well. The placing of the PRINT in the program determines when the labels will be produced. The moral here is that if you want column headings, you probably don't want the PRINT statement to be inside a loop. Print any column headings out early in the program, before setting up any looping operations.

The example illustrates the continuation of the FORMAT on a second line in the program. The need for continuing an instruction to a second or third line usually develops first when programming output labels. Remember the continuation is caused by the appearance of a non-zero numeral (or nonblank character) in column 6. As shown in the present example, the numeral 1 in column 6 of the last row causes it to become a continuation of the line before it. Practically any character appearing in column 6 would have the same effect. The continuation capability is needed whenever a FORMAT or any other statement is too long to fit within columns 7 to 72.

In addition to the control of output spacing along a row, FORMAT enables skipping rows. For example, the two division symbols at the end of the 202 FORMAT cause skipping two output lines. This provides two blank rows between the column headings and the first row of numerical output. In formatting, the Xs and the /s are similar in function. The former skip columns, the latter skip rows.

Labels and values can be intermixed in formatted output. For example, the program fragment:

```
      A = 55.6
      PRINT 106, A
106 FORMAT (1X, 'A=',F6.2)
         .
```

would yield an output row containing A= 55.60.

Frequently, when output is to be produced by line printer, the output is desired on a page separate from the page with the program listing. The simple way to do this is to FORMAT a numeral 1 in column 1's position. This causes the line printer to skip to a new page. For example, the combination:

```
      PRINT 303
303 FORMAT ('1',///,5X,'COLUMN A')
         .
```

would cause a line printer to skip to a new page, then drop down three rows, and move over five columns before printing COLUMN A. Why not try a couple of programs with formatted output?

2.20 Exercises 2-3

Facility in the use of FORMAT enables one to locate output in the desired location on an output page, and to make full use of the space available when many values are to be printed out. Use output of 1s, Xs, and /s to position and embellish your output from the following exercises.

1. Reprogram the production of a labeled multiplication table, this time using looping and FORMAT. Make the table as extensive as possible, but keep the output all on one page.

2. Program with a nested DO pair. Have the outer DO generate the even numbers from 2 to 20. Have the inner loop generate the factorials of the even numbers. Augment the output with suitable labels.

3. Adapt an example program to produce a table of square (cube, fourth) roots for even numbers from 2 to 100.

4. Adapt an example program to select 1000 integers at random. Sort the integers into descending order and determine the counts for each. Have your program identify the most frequently selected integer. Make provision to identify as many as three of these if all have the same, maximum count.

5. Use suitable labels to embellish the table of trigonometric function values or other table produced by one of your earlier programming efforts. Accommodate the values in suitable fields. The following may give you some suggestions:

```
ANGLE   ANGLE *
 DEG.    RAD.  *  SIN     COS     TAN      COT    *
********************************************************
  0.     .0000 * .0000  1.0000   .0000  TOOBIG  * 1.5708  90.
  1.     .0175 * .0175   .9998   .0175  57.299  * 1.5533  89.
  2.     .0349 * .0349   .9994   .0349  28.654  * 1.5359  88.
  .       .    *  .       .       .       .     *  .       .
  .       .    *  .       .       .       .     *  .       .
 44.     .7679 * .6947   .7193   .9657  1.0355  *  .8029  46.
 45.     .7854 * .7071   .7071  1.0000  1.0000  *  .7854  45.
        ********************************************************
              *  COS     SIN     COT      TAN   *  RAD.   DEG.
                                               * ANGLE  ANGLE
```

Hint: To get **** try FORMAT(4('*')).

6. Develop a program to generate a 4-column table showing: in column 1 all metric values from 0 to 100 by 5; in columns 2, 3, and 4, the corresponding inches, feet, and yards rounded to two decimal places. Use appropriate column headings.

7. Construct a program to print out your first and last initials in a form similar to that shown here:

```
TTTTT   BBBBB
  TT    B   B
  TT    B BBB
  TT    B   B
  TT    BBBBB
```

Output should be centered on the page. Try this exercise in both a vertical and horizontal layout on the page.

8. Use a WHILE loop to determine how many years it takes a deposit of $500 to grow to $1000 at an interest rate of 7% compounded annually. Expand your program to produce a table using formatted output showing the time required to reach $1000 for interest rates from 4 to 12% by 0.5% and initial outlays of $100, 200, . . . , 900.

9. Write a program to perform long division on pairs of integers that are read in from a file. Use the brute force approach of repeated subtraction in a WHILE loop to calculate both the integer quotient and remainder. Implement the same logic using a DO loop and GO-TO structure.

10. Write a program that uses iteration to compute the sum of the geometric series: $1 + 1/2 + 1/4 + \ldots + 1/2^{**}N$. How many terms must be summed to achieve an accuracy of 10E-09 if the exact value of the series is known to be 2.0?

2.21 INTEGER FORMAT

Although the input and output of integer quantities can be handled with free-format READ* and PRINT* instructions, any involvement with integer operations soon prompts consideration of another FORMAT. Most of us regard this as an unfortunate complication, but it is something we must face. If a program directs the output of an integer quantity and specifies an F field, then someone is doomed to disappointment. But the trouble is easily avoided by using an I field specification for the output, and the form of the field specification is not all that different. For example, when appearing within the parens of a FORMAT, the characters I9 refer to a field that will accommodate integers. Of course, the 9 means the field will be 9 columns wide. If a number were in front of the I, this would tell how many of the fields were intended. The Fortran statement:

```
36 FORMAT(1X,2I8,I4)
```

accommodates output of three integer quantities. The first two appear in eight-column fields and the third in a cozy four columns. Output in I fields appears as far to the right as possible in the specified field. We say the values are **right justified** in the field.

It is quite proper to include field specs of both F and I type in the same FORMAT statement, provided that the type of variable corresponds to the field reserved for it. The segment:

```
PRINT 84, A, K, B, I9
84 FORMAT(1X,F10.3,I6,F12.4,I2)
```

shows a sequence of field specifications that correspond in type to the variables in the PRINT list. Note that the I9 in the PRINT list is **not** the specification of a field; it is the name of an integer variable. The value of the variable will be written in a two-column field. If the value to be written out is larger than 99 or less than -9, it cannot be accommodated in the specified field and overflow may well be expected.

2.22 Alphanumeric FORMAT

Neither F-type nor I-type FORMAT can accommodate CHARACTER output. You have probably guessed by now that this is leading to yet another of Fortran's famous FORMATs. This time it is A-type, or **alphanumeric,** if you go for long, picturesque words. The field specs are practically the same as with I-type, but with A replacing the I. For example, (A6,2A8) designates three alphanumeric fields, the first is to be six columns and the other two are to be eight columns wide. The filling of these fields proceeds as does the filling of the character variables. The columns on the left are filled first, and any characters on the right have to do with the space left over.

2.23 Reading with FORMAT Control

FORMAT control of reading proves advantageous whenever we want to select values from specific locations in a data file. For example, suppose each row in a data file held values in, say, six separate fields. If we wanted to process only the values in the fourth and sixth fields, using the READ* with free-format presents some problems. Unless special provisions are made, the READ* will get its first values from the first and second fields, not the data desired. One can, of course, use extra variables to absorb the values in the fields containing unwanted data, then disregard these variables in whatever data processing is to be done. You could use variables B1, B2, B3, B4, B5, and B6 and read values from all six fields, but use only B4 and B6 in the purposeful part of the program. Most people would agree that this is a clumsy way to do business. Moreover, if any of the fields in the data file are blank or if values in adjacent fields are run together without a blank between, as sometimes happens in the world of real data files, the reading can be seriously misdirected. Perhaps you can see why echoing the data is such a good idea.

In other circumstances we may want to create as compact a data file as possible. If many small values are to be accommodated, then the need for blanks to separate the values may be objectionable. Moreover, FORMAT control of reading enables inserting the decimal points when the reading is done, so only the numbers need appear in the file. Accordingly, your consideration of reading with FORMAT control is invited. But at all times remember, if free-format well serves your programming needs, go ahead and use it.

FORMAT control of reading is quite similar to FORMAT control of printing. A number replaces the asterisk in the READ*, and the same number appears elsewhere in the program as the statement number of a FORMAT instruction. The READ and the FORMAT need not appear together in the program. In some cases the same FORMAT can be used for both reading and printing, but this isn't always advantageous.

When reading with F-type FORMAT, the field specification provides the decimal point to be included with any numbers found in the data field **as long as no decimal point appears in the field.** When reading the numerals 123 from a three-column field using (F3.2) for field specification, the value obtained will be 1.23. Inasmuch as no decimal point appears with the data, the FORMAT provides a point so that two digits appear on its right side. If a decimal point appears with the numerals in the data file, or as entered through a terminal, the decimal point overrides the FORMAT control. A decimal point appearing in a field read in under either F-type or E-type FORMAT will always govern. If no point appears in the field, the FORMAT determines where the point will be located. If two decimal points appear in a designated field, stand by for a program crash.

The following example illustrates almost all you will need to know to start using formatted reading in your own programs.

```
C
C PROGRAM ILLUSTRATING READING WITH FORMAT CONTROL
C
      READ 101, W, X, Y, Z
      READ 101, S, T, U, V
      READ 102, O, P, Q, R
      PRINT 104, W, X, Y, Z
      PRINT 104, S, T, U, V
      PRINT 104, O, P, Q, R
  101 FORMAT (4F6.1)
  102 FORMAT (F3.2,F6.5,F4.0,F1.0)
  104 FORMAT (1X,4F15.5)
      END
```

Example data:
```
12345678901234567890123456789012345678 90
12.3456.7890.1234567890.1234567890123456
12345678901234567890123456789012345678 90
```

The output produced by one implementation of Fortran is shown following the column indicators:

```
        1          2          3          4          5          6
1234567890123456789012345678901234567890123456789012345678901 2345
    12345.60000     78901.20000     34567.80000     90123.40000
       12.34500         6.78900          .12345     67890.00000
        1.23000         4.56789      123.00000           4.00000
```

The first two instructions in the example program each direct reading into four variables using the same FORMAT. Inasmuch as there are no decimal points in any of the fields in the first data row, the FORMAT controls the first READ. All values obtained are embellished with decimal points, and each point is inserted so that one of the six digits read is situated to the right of the point. This is in accordance with the F6.1 field specification.

Observe that the FORMAT for the PRINT is different from the one controlling input. In accordance with the F15.5 field specification, all output values have five digits on the right side of a decimal point. So the output FORMAT fills in four zeros for each. The second data row includes decimal points. As can be seen, the decimal points appearing in the data field override the input FORMAT. Whenever a decimal point is included with data, it will be read in just as it appears. Note that the decimal point does occupy a column in the data field, so only five digits are obtained from the F6.1 field.

The third data row is the same as the first, but the FORMAT controlling the READ is quite different. The 102 FORMAT includes fields of different widths, and specifying different locations for decimal points. The example shows how the READ can be directed to specific columns in the data row, and how decimal points can be inserted. The output FORMAT includes an X field, which directs skipping of one column. Check the output values to ensure your grasp of formatted reading.

Any attempt to read beyond the end of a data file is just as hazardous when using formatted control as when using free-format. If the data available are not sufficient to satisfy the READ, trouble is a distinct possibility. One means for protection in such instances has already been noted: the use of a fake data value as a sentinel to STOP execution or to cause transfer of control. A second approach depends on knowing in advance the number of rows in the data file. Here the number of rows of data could be read first into an integer variable, and then that variable could be used to control the remainder of the reading.

A preferred way to provide protection against attempting to read too far is to use Fortran's **other** END, one that is quite different from the one we have all grown accustomed to using as the last item in each of our programs. This END appears as part of a READ instruction and establishes the place in the program to which transfer is to be made if the READ ever runs out of data. You will soon see all this in an example. There is a similar control feature, this one named **ERR**. If you have a tendency to include decimal points in INTEGER fields, occasionally try to slip an extra decimal point in with a REAL data value, or even try to read a strange character in from either F or I fields, ERR may be just the thing you need. How about both the new END and the ERR in the same example?

```
C
C EXAMPLE READ WITH PROTECTION BUILT IN AGAINST EITHER
C READING TOO FAR, OR TOO FOUL. WHY BE ONLY HALF SAFE?
C
      DIMENSION A (10)
      READ (*,101,END=40,ERR=50) A
      PRINT 102,A
      STOP
   40 PRINT 103
      STOP
   50 PRINT 104
      STOP
  101 FORMAT (F10.2)
  102 FORMAT (1x,5F8.3)
  103 FORMAT (1X,'TRIED TO READ PAST END OF DATA')
  104 FORMAT (1X,'EVIDENT FOUL-UP IN THE DATA')
      END
```

This example shows the READ properly embellished with END and ERR within a new set of parens. The FORMAT's statement number is in there too, along with an asterisk. In the position shown, the asterisk designates standard input as it would be read from a data file tacked on or supplied to the program. If the data file is exhausted, transfer is made to statement 40 and the appropriate message is printed out. Then execution ceases. Why not try to run this gem and check out END and ERR with your own data?

When reading numerals with FORMAT control, some implementations of Fortran interpret embedded blanks as zeros. Some others do not; they squeeze out the blanks. For example, when reading 6 78, the value obtained would be 678. This can be assured by including a BN specification in the FORMAT; the blanks will not be regarded as zeros. If BZ is used, the blanks are read as zeros. For example:

```
FORMAT(BZ,F8.3,I9,BN,I4,F10.2)
```

would serve to control reading into two real and two integer variables. Any blanks encountered in the first two fields will be regarded as zeros; those in the last two fields will not.

Chances are there is little additional information you need to program reading integer data. Whenever you do, make sure that the field spec and the location of the data agree, otherwise the value established may well be off by a factor of ten or so. Under I-type control, all data values are interpreted to be right justified in the field specified. If they aren't, well let's hope you are getting in the habit of echoing the data.

Free-format quickly loses its charm when used for input of CHARACTER data. This can result, for instance, if substantial data are in machine-readable form, but without the quotation marks. Here A-type FORMAT comes to the rescue. Of course, by now you would strive to attain agreement between the number of characters a variable can accommodate and the width of the A-type field from which the value for the variable is to be obtained.

2.24 DATA

One area in which Fortran invites confusion is in the double (or even triple) use of an English-language word. Such double use of END was mentioned in the last section. Similar double use is made of the word **data.** Thus far the term has been used to refer to information separate from a program that uses it. The information can either be tacked on following the end of a program or read from a separate file. Either way, the information is distinctly separate from the program itself. But **DATA** is different. This DATA is a Fortran instruction; it belongs right in there in the program. Fortran's DATA statement provides an alternative to either assigning values to, or reading values into, variables. DATA serves best for values that will not be changed, for example, 3.14159 and the like. You may well feel that you don't need an alternative, but this one comes in handy now and then. Why not take a look at an example?

```
C
C EXAMPLE DATA STATEMENT
C
      DATA A,B,K/36.4,80.0,9/
      .
```

When appearing early in a program, this DATA statement establishes values for the three listed variables. As you can see, the variable names appear first, following the introductory DATA. The names are separated by commas and followed by a slash or division symbol. The slash introduces the values that are to be given to the variables. The values are transferred on the basis of corresponding position; the first variable gets the first value, etc. As the example shows, different types of variables can be included, but prudent programmers will strive for consistency by providing real constants for real variables, and integers for integers. They will also check to ensure that the number of data enclosed within the slashes agrees with the number of variables. The example DATA would serve to replace three assignment statements. Longer lists can be filled by continuing the DATA statement over several lines. The same data value can be provided for many variables with a form similar to multiplication within the slashes. For example:

```
C
C DATA STATEMENT SETTING THE SAME VALUES
C FOR EACH OF SEVERAL VARIABLES
C
      DATA A1,A2,A3,A4,A5/4*100.0,9.6E+04/
```

This DATA statement effectively assigns the value 100.0 to each of the first four variables in the list. Variable A5 gets a starkly different value, illustrating the use of exponential form for a constant in the DATA statement.

An implied DO loop can be used in conjunction with a DATA statement to establish initial values for part of a subscripted variable. The accompanying example shows how this works. Here the variable ZIP is dimensioned to 100 then the DATA statement establishes values for the first eight of the 100 elements in the array.

```
C
C COMBINATION OF IMPLIED DO AND DATA STATEMENT
C
      REAL ZIP(100)
      DATA (ZIP(N),N=1,8)/1.0,2.0,3.0,4.0,5.0,6.0,7.0,8.0/
      .
```

A DATA statement can serve to establish values for CHARACTER variables. But remember to include the single quotation marks with the data in the DATA statement. For example, consider the following, in the event you want to invert half your alphabet.

```
C
C EXAMPLE DATA STATEMENT FOR CHARACTER VARIABLES
C
      CHARACTER A,B,C,...M
      DATA A,B,C,...M/'Z','Y','X',...'N'/
      .
      .
```

2.25 Exercises 2-4

The mastery of level-two skills enables you to represent and deal with a wide variety of situations, some of them approaching the real world in complexity. Try your hand at one or two of these simple exercises then try one or two of the others listed later. Some will prompt your use of practically all the skills encountered thus far.

1. Prepare a program that reads from a data line similar to the first data line shown on page 75, and utilizes the data to produce the following output:

```
X = 1.234
Y = 789.0
Z = 111.1
W = 434.3
```

2. Create a file holding a haphazard group of 100 three-digit integers. Prepare a program that reads the file as data and identifies the largest and the smallest value in the group together with the positions in which the values were found. Program accommodations for up to three equal, maximum or minimum integers and provide output labels to meet all possible outcomes.

3. Read the data prepared for the previous exercise into an array. Compute the average of the 100 data values. In a second array store the differences between the values stored in the first array and the average. In a third array store the squares of the values in the second array. Sum the values in the third array. Find the square root of the average of the values in the third column; this is the standard deviation. Have your program print out the mean and the plus and minus one- and two-s.d. limits. Format appropriate labels.

4. Read characters into two 50-element arrays. Sort the characters in each array, then merge the contents of the two into a third array. Print the contents of the third array in four columns with the first output column showing the contents of elements 1 to 25, the second column the contents of elements 26 to 50, etc.

5. Create a data file consisting of a paragraph taken from one of your recent compositions. Run a program that determines the average number of letters per word and the average number of words per sentence in the paragraph.

6. Create a data file more or less in the form of a page in the phone book for a small town. Recruit assistance in making this of, say, 100 entries in the form shown:

```
Ramey,     George R.     341 Swift  St.    463-9811
Roberts,   Michael N.   1127 Perrin St.    494-6733
Rogers,    Rebecca C.    774 Knox   Rd.    747-8824
Rumbaugh,  Philip T.     455 Bleak  Pl.    452-3118
```

Prepare a program that will read in the data file and, for example, print out the data for all persons found living on the same street, or having the same first name. As another option, have your program read in an integer and a character, say '3' and 'g'; have your program select all persons for whom 'g' is the third letter in their name. For one more option, read an integer, then print out the data for all customers who have telephone numbers ending with the integer.

7. Modify the program in the example on page 56 to print the bar graphs in vertical position instead of horizontal. Don't try to print bar graphs of the test scores for everyone in a large class, have one bar represent the scores from 1.0 to 10.0, etc.

8. Modify the following program to produce a large number of values for variable RANDO; these values will be distributed between 0.0 and 1.0. Determine the counts for values found between 0.0 and 0.05, and between 0.05 and 0.99, etc. Prepare a set of 20 bar graphs for the intervals and visually check for uniformity in the distribution of the decimal fractions produced. Try different values in the data statement and see if you can improve the uniformity of the distribution.

```
C TRIAL RANDOM NUMBER GENERATOR
      DATA J,M,K/1027,3372196,3/
        XM = M
      DO 10 IR = 1,30
      K = MOD(J*K,M)
      XX = K
      RANDO = ABS(XX/XM)
      PRINT*,IR,RANDO
   10 CONTINUE
      END
```

9. Your efforts with the previous exercise yielded a rectangular distribution, the probability being reasonably uniform across the range from 0.0 to 1.0. Use the results of your previous efforts and program the generation of a triangular distribution, that is, the probability decreasing as the value 1.0 is approached.

10. Use the rectangular distribution again. This time make up sets of n values, where for the first run n has the value five. Draw sets of five values from the rectangular distribution, (randomly selected sets, of course) and compute the means for each set. Now distribute the means, plot a set of bar graphs and see if you can recognize the emerging picture.

11. Resurrect one of your previous programs that produces factorials. Add a column of output that shows the factorials with commas included between three decimal digits, as in 6,227,020,800 for factorial 13.

12. Encoding by Caesar's rundown consists of replacing each letter in the alphabet by the letter displaced by an integer that can be anything from 1 to 24. For example, if the integer were 3, then the word 'CAT' would be

encoded as 'FDW'. Run a program that tries enough offset values to decode the following vital messages:

```
AOL YHPU PU ZWHPU ZAHFZ THPUSF VU AOL WSHPU
RFC OSGAI ZPMUL DMV HSKNCB MTCP RFC JYXW BME
LQJWLNB JAN CQRB RB VXAN CQJW NWXDPQ OXACAJW
```

2.26 Summary for Level Two

As envisioned here, level-two programmers will confidently use three of Fortran's data types, declaring variables and nimbly exchanging type as advantage dictates. They will demonstrate use of singly subscripted variables, both for output and input and for data processing within a program. All will readily manage multiple looping both with counter and condition control. Finally, our level-two programmers will usually favor FORMAT control of standard input and output; they will use F and I field specifications with confidence and E and A fields without trepidation. By now type-consistent operations, adequate commenting, and echoing data will have become habitual.

In some contrast to the transition between a first and second level of programming skill, transition to a third level does not merit unqualified recommendation for all. For some occasional programmers, mastery of the skills represented here as a second level may signal a point of diminishing returns. The additional power offered by the programming elements yet to come may not prove worthwhile, especially if they are to be used only infrequently. All should recognize that any feasible programming task can be done with level-two skills. For some, the level-two skills practiced with confidence may be the optimum choice.

Chapter 3

Toward Powerful Programming

The toughest thing to learn is that a better way may not necessarily be the optimum way.　　　　　　　—Disgruntled Student

Several major items remain to be included in anyone's catalog of Fortran elements. Establishing the initial contacts with them becomes a primary objective for those who want to advance their programming potential. In comparison with capabilities considered thus far, those considered next offer the potential for increased power and convenience. With the increased power and convenience comes increased hazard for the occasional programmer.

Although the great majority of programming can be handled with the Fortran represented here as characteristic of intermediate skill, the topics of multiple subscripts and user subprograms are so widely applicable and offer such substantial advantage that all who program should be aware of their existence. Most will benefit from some practice with each and many will soon find that one or both merit the effort needed to develop confidence in their use. Next for consideration is the fourth of Fortran's data types, LOGICAL. Although serviceable on its own, it may be of more value in combinations that enable programming multiple-consideration and multiple-alternative decisions. Two more data types, DOUBLE PRECISION and COMPLEX round out Fortran's data handling capabilities. Few neophytes will have frequent need for these, but until they are identified, our picture of Fortran is incomplete.

For many initiates, programmed management of files is destined to become a primary consideration. Notwithstanding the likely importance, some allowance must be made presently for variations between systems. The present level of system dependence evidently precludes definitive treatment that is universally applicable.

Several odds and ends follow. Some have been a part of Fortran for a long time, whereas others are of more recent origin, yet all may hold potential for only infrequent service. After establishing the contact, developing the programmer's judgment of the likelihood of advantage and of hazard may well be the paramount consideration.

3.1 Subscripted Variables II, Double Subscripts

The great convenience offered by singly subscripted variables has probably made you wonder about double subscripts, or subscripts of even higher order. No matter what order, a DIMENSION statement or its equivalent must precede any use of the subscripted variable. For example, either:

```
DIMENSION Z(6,4)
```

or:

```
REAL Z(6,4)
```

reserves 24 locations under the variable name Z. Think of a corresponding algebraic or geometric array. Try to associate the first subscript, here the 6, with the row dimension, and the second subscript with the number of columns in the array. Individual locations in the array are identified by their row and column index values. $Z(5,3)$ for example, designates the array element in row 5 and in column 3.

When programming with arrays, it is frequently necessary to clear all elements to zero. This can be readily done using nested DO loops, one loop for each subscript.

```
C
C EXAMPLE USE OF NESTED DO PAIR TO
C CLEAR ALL ELEMENTS IN ARRAY Z TO ZERO
C
      REAL Z(6,4)
      DO 25 IR =1,6
         DO 15 IC =1,4
            Z(IR,IC) = 0.0
   15    CONTINUE
   25 CONTINUE
```

Here the DO 25 loop is the outer loop. As it assumes control, the row index is set to 1 and control passed to the inner loop. The range of the inner, DO 15 loop is now executed four times, and then control is returned to the outer loop. Next the row index IR is advanced to 2, and the inner loop entered a second time. Each time the inner loop acts to set all four elements in a row to zero, thus clearing out the array one row at a time. The outer loop causes the inner loop to do its thing six times, once for each row in the array. The array could be cleared a column at a time by interchanging the IR = 1,6 with the IC = 1,4.

Doubly subscripted variables enhance a programmer's ability to accommodate and manipulate large amounts of information. This is especially so with respect to input and output. For example, the combination:

```
DIMENSION M(100,10)
READ 5,M
```

sets the stage for reading 1000 integer data values. Most programmers will appreciate this. However, we should consider the order in which the array will now be filled. Of course, the first data value will find its way into location $M(1,1)$. Note carefully that $M(2,1)$ is the next location to receive a value. Filling continues in this order, advancing the row index each time a location is filled, until all 100 locations in the first column have been filled. The first index, the row index, is advanced through its entire range before the second index is incremented. The same ordering is followed in similar applications of higher order subscripts unless the programmer assumes control of the subscripts. Think of the index nearest the variable controlling its inside loop, the one varying most quickly. The farther away from the name, that is, the farther outside the loop, the more slowly the index changes.

If we want to fill the array in a different order, we must program a different sequence of subscripts. If, for example, we want to read into three rows of the example M array, but read first into all ten locations of the first row, etc., then the following combination of DOs could serve.

```
DO 35 IR = 1,3
    READ 55, (M(IR,IC),IC = 1,10)
35 CONTINUE
```

This combination uses a regular DO to attend to each of the first three rows, and an implied DO to obtain the values for all ten locations in each row. If the implied DO were replaced by a regular DO, each data value would have to be on a different line.

For a further example, suppose we want to write out the contents of rows 3 to 8 and columns 6 to 10 in array M. This time let's consider nested, implied DOs.

```
PRINT 66, ((M(IR,IC),IC = 6,10),IR = 3,8)
```

The outer index is set first to its initial value; here, IR is set to 3. Then control passes to the inner loop, and index IC is cycled through the range designated. After the inner loop has completed, control returns to the outer loop. IR is advanced to four, and the inner loop reentered. As illustrated here, the inner index, the one closest to the subscripted variable, cycles through its designated range of values six times as the outer index takes on values from 3 to 8.

Quite apart from the convenience for input and output, arrays are of considerable utility for processing information within a program and for representing the information in compact form. The summary of the performance of several salesmen may provide a suitable example. Consider a two-dimensional array to hold the monthly sales for the group of salesmen. Suppose we want to summarize the tabulated values by checking the average monthly sales for each person.

	Pete	Sam	Table of Monthly Sales Fran	.	.	Ralph
Jan.	3649.12	1893.80	.	.	.	4166.34
Feb.	4308.67	5112.45	.	.	.	6144.20
Mar.	2788.19	3608.64	.	.	.	3582.86
.	.	.	.	.	.	.
Dec.	6711.44	7084.93	.	.	.	.

If the dollar amounts of each individual's sales are listed by month, as indicated in the accompanying table, then the programmer's task is first to produce the desired results for one salesperson, as represented in one array column, then repeat the operation for as many columns as necessary. For purposes of the present example let's use a real array with one row for each month, and enough columns to accommodate as many as 20 persons. Accordingly the dimensions of the array will be 12 rows by 20 columns. Singly subscripted variables are established to accumulate the sums of monthly sales and for the averages. Inasmuch as the number of persons represented is less than the column dimension of the doubly subscripted variable, the program starts off by reading in an integer that establishes the number of salesmen.

```
      C
      C PROGRAM TO SUMMARIZE ANNUAL SALES FOR STAFF OF UP TO 20 PERSONS
      C
            REAL SALES (12,20),SUM(20),AVG(20)
            READ*, N
            DO 10 IR = 1,12
               READ*, (SALES(IR,IC),IC=1,N)
      10    CONTINUE
            DO 20 IC = 1,N
               SUM(IC) = 0.0
               DO 16 IR = 1,12
                  SUM(IC) = SUM(IC) + SALES(IR ,IC)
      16       CONTINUE
               AVG(IC) = SUM(IC)/12.0
      20    CONTINUE
            PRINT 101, (AVG(IX),IX=1,N)
      101   FORMAT(/,1X,20F6.0)
            END
```

Reading in the data is next done by the implied DO nested inside the DO 10 loop. Then the DO 20 loop initializes one element in SUM to 0.0 and the DO 16 loop adds up the 12 month's sales for one person. As soon as this loop finishes, the average of the monthly sales is computed and assigned to the appropriate location in AVG. When the DO 20 loop has completed, the N averages are printed out in a row. This example illustrates a two-dimensional array at work. As you can see the array responds to operations performed in nested DOs and, as illustrated here, often works in conjunction with singly subscripted arrays matching either the row or the column dimensions. No doubt you can see how this program could be extended, for example, by summing the contents in the N locations in SUM, then dividing by REAL(N) to get the average for the entire staff.

A second example based on the same two-dimensional array will illustrate searching each row for the largest monthly sales, then preserving the sales amount and an integer designating the salesman in one-dimensional arrays. The data are read in as in the previous example, then all elements in SMAX are cleared to 0.0. The DO 50 controls searching each of the twelve rows and the DO 45 loop searches for the maximum in each row. Each time the inner loop finishes, a row maximum has been captured in the IRth element of SMAX and the integer designating the person in the corresponding element of PERSON. After variable BIGEST is set to zero the DO 60 loop searches the SMAX array and captures the maximum monthly sales together with integers designating the salesperson and the month in which the grandest sales were made.

```
      C
      C PROGRAM TO DETERMINE THE BEST MONTHLY SALES FOR EACH PERSON AND
      C THEN TO IDENTIFY THE HIGHEST MONTHLY SALES AND THE PERSON
      C
            REAL SALES (12,20),SMAX(12),BIGEST
            INTEGER PERSON (20),CHAMP,MONTH
            READ*, N
            DO 10 IR = 1,12
               READ*, (SALES(IR,IC),IC=1,N)
      10    CONTINUE
            DO 40 IR = 1.12
               SMAX(IR) = 0.0
      40    CONTINUE
            DO 50 IR = 1,12
               DO 45 IC = 1,N
                  IF(SMAX(IR) .LT. SALES(IR,IC)) THEN
                     SMAX(IR) = SALES(IR,IC)
                     PERSON(IR) = IC
                  ENDIF
      45    CONTINUE
      50    CONTINUE
            BIGEST = 0.0
            DO 60 IR = 1,12
               IF(BIGEST .LT. SMAX(IR)) THEN
                  BIGEST = SMAX(IR)
                  CHAMP = PERSON(IR)
                  MONTH = IR
               ENDIF
      60    CONTINUE
            DO 70 IR = 1,12
               PRINT 101, PERSON(IR),SMAX(IR)
      70    CONTINUE
            PRINT 102, CHAMP, MONTH, BIGEST
      101   FORMAT(1X,I10,F10.2,/)
      102   FORMAT(/,1X,' GRAND CHAMPION:',I6,
          2          /,1X,' BEST MONTH    :',I6,
          3          /,1X,' MONTHLY SALES :',F10.2)
            END
```

Let's hope you are already thinking of ways to improve this example, say by using suitable character arrays for the persons' names and the months, so the sales manager wouldn't have to decode integer values to identify the champion and the month in which he or she did best.

3.2 Graphic Output with Double Subscripts

The program at hand illustrates the use of a doubly subscripted variable for producing graphic output. The declaration establishes variable **GRID** as a character array of 31 rows by 51 columns. Next, character variables **BLANK** and **SYMBOL** are assigned suitable character constants. Following this, a pair of nested DO loops is used to blank out the array. This is similar to clearing a real or an integer array to zero before beginning computation. If only one set of points were to be plotted, or if a real array were to be used for only one computation, blanking or clearing to zero might not be essential. But if an array is to be used and then reused for a second set of points or a second computation, blanking or clearing is necessary.

Just as with manual plotting, we must decide the largest and the smallest values to be accommodated. The program shows these values to be read in with FORMAT control. Next, a loop is established to read in pairs of data values. Each pair is read in with the same FORMAT and any negative value read in for X causes transfer to the output section of the program. If negative values were to be plotted, some other value would necessarily be used for the sentinel. Evidently the assumption has been made that all data pairs will fit within the limits set by the values read in for XMIN and XMAX, etc. In such instances, a prudent programmer provides a check to make sure the values read in are within the established limits.

```
C
C EXAMPLE PROGRAM TO READ IN DATA PAIRS AND PLOT
C CORRESPONDING POINTS IN A 2-DIMENSION ARRAY
C
      CHARACTER GRID(31,51),BLANK,SYMBOL
C
C SET VALUES FOR BLANK AND SYMBOL
C
      BLANK = ' '
      SYMBOL = 'X'
C
C BLANK OUT THE ARRAY 'GRID'
C
      DO 10 IR = 1,31
         DO 5 IC = 1,51
            GRID(IR,IC) = BLANK
    5    CONTINUE
   10 CONTINUE
```

Program continued on next page.

```
C
C READ IN THE LIMITING VALUES
C
      READ 100, XMIN,XMAX,YMIN,YMAX
C
C READ IN ONE DATA PAIR
C
      DO 99 IX = 1,1000
         READ 100, X,Y
C
C IF SENTINEL VALUE FOUND IN X, GO TO OUTPUT
C
         IF(X.LT.0.0) GOTO 50
C
C COMPUTE COLUMN INDEX FOR THE POINT
C
         ICOL = ((X-XMIN)/(XMAX-XMIN))*50.0 + 1.0
C
C COMPUTE ROW INDEX FOR THE POINT
C
         IROW = 31.0 - ((Y-YMIN)/(YMAX-YMIN))*30.0
C
C PUT ONE SYMBOL IN ARRAY 'GRID' AT THE LOCATION
C CORRESPONDING TO THE DATA PAIR READ IN, THEN
C TRANSFER TO READ IN ANOTHER DATA PAIR
C
         GRID(IROW,ICOL) = SYMBOL
   99 CONTINUE
C
C OUTPUT SECTION, SKIP TO A NEW PAGE AND PRINT OUT THE
C WHOLE ARRAY 'GRID' WITH A NIFTY BORDER OF ASTERISKS
C
   50 PRINT 101
      PRINT 102
      DO 70 IR = 1,31
         PRINT 103, (GRID(IR,IC),IC=1,51)
   70 CONTINUE
      PRINT 102
      STOP
C
C FORMAT SECTION
C
  100 FORMAT(4F10.5)
  101 FORMAT('1')
  102 FORMAT(4x,53('*'))
  103 FORMAT(4x,'*',51A1,'*')
      END
```

The computations of the row and column indices are done with reals and then the results assigned to integers. Reals must be used for the computation, and integers are needed for the subscripts that are to locate the point in the array. Assignment of the result of the real computation to an integer may prompt a caution message from some compilers. If so, an extra step involving the integer function INT would provide relief. The computation of the column index is consistent with the number of columns established for the array. The fraction that results from the division, when multiplied by 50.0, always yields values from 0.0 to 50.0. The 1.0 added on protects against the column index ever becoming zero. Thus the resulting index is always between 1 and 51. Computation of the row index includes a reversal to accommodate the difference between conventional representation of rows in arrays and their representation in Cartesian coordinates. In arrays the first row is interpreted to be on top, but in Cartesian coordinates it is at the bottom. Once values for ICOL and IROW are established, the designated element of the array is assigned the value held by SYMBOL, and transfer is made to read in a new data pair.

The output section first directs printing a numeral 1 in column 1's position. This causes the line printer to skip to a new page, so the plot will appear on an output page by itself. Next, an implied DO is nested within an ordinary DO to print the array suitably. Each output row is embellished with asterisks at each end, and a stunning row of asterisks is printed to close the top and the bottom.

3.3 Exercises for Double Subscripts

Many contemporary students encounter arrays, or subscripted variables, for the first time in their pursuit of computer programming. This occurs because, in the customary sequence of mathematics instruction, an introduction to arrays comes in the third or fourth semester of collegiate study. So, if your introduction to arrays seems unduly abrupt, rest assured your position is reasonable. Remember too, you can do with single subscripts practically anything that can be done with double subscripts, so in your pursuit of this set of exercises, if you have a strong preference, you could use only singles. But inasmuch as you have come this far, why not give doubles a try? And as you do keep thinking: *row-column, row-column.*

Use the accompanying array of names and bowling scores for data for related exercises in this set.

Scores for the XYZ Bowling Team

Name	Score 1	Score 2	Score 3	Score 4	Score 5	Score 6
Dan Achin	163	111	147	104	179	140
Don Ewing	189	166	172	118	137	149
Kitt Baumhoer	121	167	189	116	142	186
Anne Heiser	114	178	181	172	168	204
Ron Beeson	186	162	178	129	155	174
Jean Aylor	149	142	178	181	189	211
Pete Bradshaw	163	117	149	184	176	153
Lori Mack	139	176	134	146	177	183
Grant Beecher	177	184	167	149	119	174
Paula Gaffney	163	171	121	144	186	179

1. Run a program that reads in the essential information and produces the following: the high and the low score for each bowler, an ordered list of the three bowlers with the highest averages and the names of the most consistent and the least consistent bowlers.

2. Given that three games are bowled on each of two meetings, perform computations that could help decide whether the team scores higher and/or more consistently during the later games.

3. Sort the entire array of scores and of names in order of descending average score. Be sure that all individual scores and the names get sorted with the averages.

4. Run a program that reads in an integer from 1 to 6, or more if you augment the data. Use the value read in to identify one column of scores and sort the entire array in descending order of the selected column.

5. Fill a 25 row by 4 column array with randomly selected letters. Sort the rows into alphabetical order using variables capable of holding only single characters. Try sorting the array by ascending order of the fourth column, then the third column, etc.

6. The example plotting program on page 87 shows evidence of origin during the 'dark ages' in which both input and output were transmitted by punched cards. The array size (31,51) was adopted because of the limit imposed by the 80-column cards. Modify the example program to make use of a full page as produced by a line printer. Plot two or more intersecting straight lines and a slant line that intersects both the other lines. Use a unique symbol for plotting the points of intersection. Include some protection against attempting to plot points outside the established ranges.

7. Modify your plot program by interchanging the axes. Have the x-axis run down the page and the y-axis run across. Extend your plot over two or three output pages.

8. Run a program that reads in two x-y data pairs and plots the line joining the two points. Have your program adjust the plotting range so the plotted line extends over more than half the x- and the y-range.

9. Run a program that plots two or three concentric circles.

10. Extend one of your plotting programs to produce a representation of Y=SQRT(X). Have your program shade in the area under the curve and between X=2.0 and X=4.0.

3.4 User Subprograms

By this time most participants will have used one or another of Fortran's standard library functions. These are **subprograms** which have been prepared by others to perform jobs frequently encountered by practically all programmers. Subprograms are programs that ordinarily do not operate by themselves. They perform their designated operation only when directed to do so by a request received from another program. The program that initiates the request is referred to as the **main** or **calling** program. This distinction gets somewhat blurred because, as you will see, subprograms can call other subprograms, and the most elementary subprograms can be regarded as intrinsic parts of their main program.

So at first encounter, the topic can seem depressingly jumbled, and the potential advantages of preparing their own subprograms escape the notice of many novice programmers. However, substantial advantages accrue to those who develop even minimal skill in preparing their own subprograms. First, there is the obvious advantage of preparing a section of code that can be used over and over by simply including a subprogram name in a Fortran operation. Next, the advantage that many dedicated programmers deem truly great, is the potential for organizing any substantial programming task in separate parts, where each identifiable part is to be done by a subprogram. This advantage may be more evident when several programmers are involved in a project, but it can be significant for an individual programmer. When you use subprograms effectively, main programs frequently do little other than request the services of subprograms.

In form, the library functions are intermediate among the three types of user subprograms. The most elementary of these is the **arithmetic statement function**, or simply **statement function**. This is limited to only one statement and is included within the main program. The intermediate form is referred to as a **function subprogram**. This can include any practical number of statements and is separate from the main program. Most library functions are of this form. Finally, there is a smashing version, the **subroutine.** This one does it all and, unless something untoward develops, will probably become your favorite.

3.5 User Subprograms I, Statement Functions

Suppose you were concerned with a program that has recurrent need for a one-statement computation. Of course, you could duplicate the instruction at each place the computation was needed, but, if the needs were numerous and the statement was involved, you probably would begin to think of better ways. One better way to satisfy the requirement would be with an arithmetic statement function. When one of these is used, the calculation is programmed in only one place and is then invoked wherever needed in the program by simply using the function name in the operation part of a Fortran statement. Sounds simple, doesn't it? The Fortran statement:

```
AREA(S,A,B,C) = SQRT(S*(S-A)*(S-B)*(S-C))
```

provides an example of a statement function. This one grinds out the area of a triangle if it is given the three sides and the value of S, which, in case you have forgotten, is half their sum. If this statement function were to appear early in a program before any executable statements but after declarations then, after values have been established for variables P, D, A, B, and C, we could use:

```
.
S = (A+B+C)/2.0
WK = P*D*AREA(S,A,B,C)
.
```

This establishes a value for variable S in the main part of the program and then activates the statement function called AREA. We say that the function is **called** when its name appears in the operation part of an instruction. Control is then transferred to the function. After the function has finished, control comes back to the point from which the call was made.

The several variables used in establishing the function are referred to as **parameters.** These may be regarded as dummy variables because the values with which the indicated calculation is to be performed are not yet established. When values are established in the main part of the program for transfer to the function, the values are assigned to variables identified as **arguments.** The values held by the arguments are then transferred to the statement function. The transfers are always made on the basis of corresponding position; the first argument is substituted for the first parameter, etc. Upon transfer to the function, the argument values are substituted for the corresponding parameters and the function's job is done. The result then goes back to the spot from which the initial transfer was made.

The arguments need not have the same names as the parameters. The previous example shows the same variable names used for arguments in the calling statement (WK=P*D*AREA . . .) and for corresponding parameters in the statement function. The first argument in the calling statement is variable S, and the first parameter in the statement list is also S, etc. However, when one puts a statement function to use, different names can be used as arguments. The only requirement is that the argument names and the parameter names agree in type. For instance, the segment:

```
.
B = (X+A+3.5)/2.0
WK = P*D*AREA(B,X,A,3.5)
```

invokes the statement function as well and shows the independence regarding variable names. The use of the variable names B and A in the main part of the program is quite different from their use in the statement function. In the second example, the value established for variable B in the main part of the program is effectively transferred to the location(s) of variable S in the statement function. Always remember, the transfers are made on the basis of corresponding position; the naming of arguments is independent of the naming of parameters. You can see that this takes some getting used to. But you can also see that statement functions can be handy to have around.

3.6 User Subprograms II, Function Subprograms

Although they can be very helpful, statement functions have limitations. In general their use is limited to relatively simple chunks of calculation. Of course, you could make up a hefty statement function by continuing it on several lines of code if you were careful to balance all those parens. But the truth is that programmers, real programmers, use several or even many short instructions in preference to long, involved instructions. And the statement function is limited to a single Fortran statement. Too bad about that, but that is why we have function subprograms. Function subprograms allow the programmer to use any number of program statements. They are independent of the main program insofar as the naming of variables and the numbering of statements are concerned. Function subprograms are more powerful than statement functions, so, as you have probably surmised, they are a bit more involved to set up.

First, function subprograms, or simply **functions** are truly **sub**programs. They are separate from or external to the main program that uses them. Initiating transfer to a function subprogram is easy; it is practically the same as arranging for transfer to a statement function. In either case, the subprogram name appears in the operation part of a program instruction, together with one or more arguments. When any subprogram is called into action, a transfer of control takes place. If an arithmetic statement function is used, the transfer of control does not go outside the bounds of the main program. The transfer is internal within the main program. After an arithmetic statement function finishes its job, the subsequent return of control is automatic. Control is always returned to the operation in which the subprogram name appeared. When library functions or user function subprograms are used, a transfer is made outside, or external to the bounds of the main program. Accordingly, in comparison with return from a statement function, the return of control from a function subprogram is just a bit more involved.

When return is to be made from a function subprogram to the calling program, the computer needs prompting. It needs to be told to return. This too is easy. The Fortran instruction is (you probably guessed it) RETURN. You see, this is the price we pay for being able to use several statements in the function. When only one operation is to be performed, as there necessarily is when using an arithmetic statement function, the computer knows it should return as soon as the function is done. But function subprograms can hold many instructions, and the poor computer might not know for sure whether to carry on within the function subprogram or go back to the calling program unless the signal to RETURN were given.

Finally, the function subprogram is a sub**program**. As such, it has a specific beginning and end. The beginning is the word FUNCTION and the end is END. The skeleton for a function subprogram is ready, are you?

```
      FUNCTION SAM(A,B,C)
C
C SKELETON FUNCTION SUBPROGRAM
C
      . . .
      . . .
      SAM =...
      . . .
      RETURN
      END
```

This representation shows the essential characteristics of a function subprogram. It starts with FUNCTION, and this is followed by a suitable name. The name is followed by a set of parens, and these hold the dummy variables or parameters. These are the variables used to set up the function. The body of the function has been represented by dots here to emphasize the next feature. In at least one statement in the function, the name of the function must appear alone on the left side of an equals sign. The name can appear in more than one such statement, but it must appear in at least one. Next, there must be at least one RETURN instruction. There can be many, but there must be at least one. Finally, the end of the function is established by our old friend END. Remember, the function is a program, and all Fortran programs must end with END. All the instructions that make up the function are usually placed in sequence immediately following the END of the main program.

An example showing a function and its relation to a main program may be in order. This first shows a part, and then the END of the main program followed by the function.

```
C
C THIS PART REPRESENTS THE MAIN PROGRAM
C
      .
      WK = P*D*AREA(X,Y,Z)
      .
      END
C
C THE FUNCTION FOLLOWS THE END
C      OF THE MAIN PROGRAM
C
      FUNCTION AREA (A,B,C)
C
C HERE IS THE FUNCTION SUBPROGRAM
C
      S = (A+B+C)/2.0
      AREA = SQRT(S*(S-A)*(S-B)*(S-C))
      RETURN
      END
```

Here we presume that values for X, Y, and Z have been established in the main, or call-ing, program. These values are transferred to the function and inserted wherever the corresponding parameters appear. The correspondence is established based on the variables' positions in the two lists, that is, the argument list in the main program (X,Y,Z) and the parameter list in the function (A,B,C). The example shows that the naming of a corresponding pair of variables is independent, though it is essential to use the same variable type. The default type for both variables X and A is real, so they can refer to the same location in memory and establish the necessary transfer. Real arguments must be passed to real parameters, and integers to integers. Programmers who are inclined to use pairs like X and M in such situations should plan on extra time for debugging their programs.

Besides the independence in the use of variable names, the statement numbers used within a function subprogram are independent of the numbers used in the call-ing program. You can use the same number as a statement number in the calling program and as a statement number in the function. So what's wrong with functions? Well, they are intended for returning only one value to the calling program, the value associated with the name of the function. If a particular task required the calculation of two quantities, two function subprograms would be needed. As you will see shortly, subroutines are not limited in this way.

3.7 User Subprograms III, Subroutines

If by now you have experienced satisfaction in running a program or two with statement functions and function subprograms, you should be ready to go all the way with a subroutine. The form of a subroutine is quite similar to that of a function. Of course, the former begins with SUBROUTINE followed by the subroutine name. The other obvious difference is in the calling statement. When seeking to invoke any function, you simply call it by name. But in order to capitalize on the magic of a subroutine, you must use the Fortran instruction CALL. For example:

```
C
C EXAMPLE PROGRAM WITH USER SUBROUTINE
C
      .
      .
      CALL AREA (S,X,Y,Z,BB)
      WK = P*D*BB
      .
      END
C
C THAT WAS THE MAIN, OR CALLING PROGRAM
C      THE SUBROUTINE COMES NEXT
C
      SUBROUTINE AREA(S,A,B,C,AA)
C
C THIS IS THE EXAMPLE SUBROUTINE
C
      S = (A + B + C)/2.0
      AA = SQRT(S*(S-A)*(S-B)*(S-C))
      RETURN
      END
```

This time assume that values have been established for variables X, Y, and Z in the main program before the CALL. These values are transferred to the subroutine and become values for variables A, B, and C, respectively. Keep in mind the requirement to use the same type of variable on both sides of this transfer. Don't use variable I in the calling program in the position corresponding to variable B in the subroutine, etc. After transfer is made to the subroutine, the values of A, B, and C are used to establish a value for variable S. Then AA is calculated, and return is made to the calling program. The neat feature here is that values are now available for variables S and BB in the calling program. We say variables S and BB were empty when the CALL was made. Values for the corresponding variables are established in the subroutine, so after return the same values are available in the main program.

The example shows variable S in the calling program to be in the position corresponding to variable S in the subroutine. Any other real variable name could have been used in the CALL statement; that would then be the variable to which the value of S was returned. Similarly BB in the calling program corresponds to AA in the subroutine. Both S and AA are empty when the call is made. Both contain appropriate values after the RETURN is made. Observe that the subprogram name necessarily does **not** appear to the left of an equals sign as it does in the function subprogram. Another minor consideration concerns the place to which return is made. When using a subroutine, the return is made to the main program statement next following the CALL.

3.8 Subprogram Exercises

1. Show that you can use a simple arithmetic statement function by running a program that uses the statement function to add three real values together and returns the sum to the main program for output.

2. Prepare a program that reads in the value of angles expressed in degrees. Use an arithmetic statement function to convert degrees to radians. Demonstrate the function's operation with ten data values.

3. Run a main program that uses two arithmetic statement functions. A real number is transferred each time one of the functions is invoked. The same value is transferred to each function. The first function returns the reciprocal of the transferred number in decimal fraction form. The second returns the value of one minus the decimal fraction returned by the first function. Read In ten suitable data values and have your program print out the data values together with the two decimal fractions.

4. Run a program that reads numerical data accompanied by a three character string, either *psi* or *nsm*. If the input value is in pounds per square inch (psi) transfer to the first arithmetic statement function, if the input value is in newtons per square meter (nsm) transfer to the second function. Have both functions return values in *torr*, (millimeters of mercury) for output.

5. Prepare a program that uses a function subprogram using two real values as arguments. If the first of the two is larger than the second have the function return the sum of the two. If the second is larger return the absolute value of the difference. If the difference between the two arguments is less than 1.0E-03, have the function return the value zero.

6. Run a program that reads in three real values and transfers them as arguments to a function subprogram. Have the function determine whether the three values could be the sides of a triangle. Return either an integer one or two for the main program to decode. Have the main program print out the three values and the string 'TRIANGLE' or 'NO TRIANGLE' as appropriate.

7. Use a subroutine instead of the two arithmetic statement functions of exercise 4. Have the subroutine determine the units of the data value by examining the accompanying characters, then make appropriate unit conversions and return the pressure for output by the main program. Output the pressure expressed in three different units, that is, if read in using nsm, output is to include the nsm value and the equivalent psi and torr.

8. Program a loop that produces a sequence of positive real numbers beginning with 0.1 or less and extending to values greater than ten. Have the main program call a subroutine that will interpret the argument to be either the cosine or the secant of some angle. Have the subroutine return the value of the angle in degrees, together with a suitable character string indicating how the argument was interpreted.

3.9 Arrays as Subprogram Arguments

To this point the examples have shown transfer between main programs and subprograms via individual variables. These appear in lists, one list in the main program and a corresponding list in the subprogram. When many variables are to be transferred, almost any clear-thinking programmer would begin wondering how a subscripted variable or two might be of help. If you find yourself thinking along these lines, you are in line for a clear-thinking award. Let's hope the next example makes all this perfectly clear:

```
C
C EXAMPLE MAIN PROGRAM USING AN ARRAY IN THE CALL
C
      CHARACTER*12, BIRD(10)
      CALL CAGE (BIRD,N)
      PRINT *,N
      DO 10 J = 1,N
         PRINT*, BIRD(J)
   10 CONTINUE
      STOP
      END
C
C NEXT COMES THE SUBROUTINE
C
      SUBROUTINE CAGE (PEEP,M)
      CHARACTER*12, PEEP(10)
      READ*, M
      DO 10 K = 1,M
         READ 101, PEEP(K)
   10 CONTINUE
      RETURN
  101 FORMAT (A12)
      END
```

This example illustrates several features, but let's attend to the current one first. The first line in the main program establishes BIRD as a ten-element array of type

CHARACTER. It further specifies each element in the array to be capable of accommodating 12 individual characters. Next, by including the array name BIRD in the CALL list, the stage is set to transfer ten 12-character variables over to the subroutine. Of course, all these as well as variable N are empty when the CALL goes out.

Turning quickly to SUBROUTINE CAGE, we observe ordinary-looking PEEP and M in the parameter list. The key to success here is in the next statement. The declaration establishes PEEP to be subscripted and of the desired type and size to correspond to BIRD. It is essential that all arrays passed to a subroutine be declared as arrays in the subroutine as well as in the main program. Passing entire arrays to single variables just does not work.

By now, you probably suspect what is going to happen. First, an integer value is read into variable M using free-format. Then a DO loop is set up to read in the number of PEEPs designated by the value read in for M. Upon return to the main program, control goes to the PRINT* which produces the number of BIRDs or PEEPs that have been CAGEd. If all goes well, the DO loop in the main program then prints out the names that were read by the DO loop in the subroutine.

The example confirms the subroutine's ability to handle input of data; output is processed as well. Take advantage of the opportunity provided by the example to review DO loops; both loops here have a variable for the upper limit of the control variable. This makes the loops adaptable to different numbers of data, but also enables exceeding the dimensions established for BIRD and PEEP. With the prompt provided by this example, make a point to recall all those good things about A-type FORMAT. If such had not been used, all the bird names in the data would have necessarily been enclosed in single quotes. Finally, note that when using a single-field input FORMAT each data entry must appear on a different line in the data file.

Probably you have already planned to use subprograms to call other subprograms. An earlier example shows a subroutine calling a supplied function. The word calling comes naturally here even though a CALL is not involved. The same arrangement is possible with user subprograms. Almost any combination of one subprogram calling another is permitted, but if difficulty arises, print out values before and after transfer to see what is going on.

A final note about subprograms. You probably expect that they follow the END of the calling program. This order is fine, however subprograms and the calling program can follow in any order. Your compiler can handle many of these without becoming confused.

3.10 Subprograms with Adjustable Arrays

As individuals become more deeply involved in programming, they usually accumulate a collection of subprograms that are especially appropriate for situations frequently encountered. In a way, the subprograms correspond to favorite tools in a mechanic's tool box. But for the programmer there is an advantage in keeping the subprograms as general as possible. One way to keep a subprogram general is to utilize Fortran's capacity for establishing the size of subprogram arrays using information passed along in the arguments. We say the dimensions of a subprogram array are adjusted to agree with the array size set in the main program. The adjustable feature holds only for arrays in subprograms, not for those in main programs. And, for practical purposes, the adjusting is prudently restricted to one-dimensional arrays.

The accompanying example shows how this works. The main program first reads an integer into variable M. The value for M in turn establishes the number of data values read into array SET. Note carefully, the value of M does **not** establish the size of the array SET; the dimension is determined by the integer 100 there in the declaration. Don't try to be general regarding the size of an array in a main program; the dimension must be an integer constant.

```
C
C THIS IS THE MAIN PROGRAM
C
      REAL SET(100)
      READ*, M
      DO 10 IC=1,M
         READ*, SET(IC)
10    CONTINUE
      ANS = STAND(SET,M)
      PRINT*, ' STANDARD DEVIATION =', ANS
      END
C
C FUNCTION SUB PROGRAM WITH ADJUSTABLE DIMENSIONS
C
      FUNCTION STAND (X,M)
      DIMENSION X(M)
      SUM = 0.0
      SUMSQ = 0.0
      DO 10 IR=1,M
         SUM = SUM + X(IR)
         SUMSQ = SUMSQ + X(IR)*X(IR)
10    CONTINUE
      VAR = ((SUMSQ - SUM*SUM/REAL(M))/REAL(M-1))
      STAND = SQRT(VAR)
      RETURN
      END
```

After the main program reads in the data, transfer is made to the subprogram with the array SET and the value in M as arguments. Observe that, until the value of M is transferred, there is no clue in the subprogram about the size of array X. Array X will now be adjusted to satisfy the requirements of the main program. Any integer up to 100 read into variable M controls the number of data values read in and the effective size of the X array in the subprogram. If, in an alternative main program the array is dimensioned 2000, then the subprogram array will accommodate any up to 2000 values. And if another main program were to use an array with dimension six, the subprogram will not be burdened with a large and substantially unused array. Note how the present example differs from the one in the previous section. There the array PEEP is inflexibly dimensioned 10 in the subroutine. With this set in the subprogram, array PEEP can never accommodate more than 10 values. And if a different main program were to use an array dimensioned three, then the subprogram would necessarily be burdened with seven elements that would not be used.

3.11 INTRINSIC and EXTERNAL

Another way to keep your subprograms general is to make them capable of calling different subprograms in turn, with the direction of the second call determined by information sent from the main program to the first-called subprogram. The present example shows how all this works out. As you can see, the main program calls subroutine SUB1 three times. Look ahead and you will see that SUB1 is set up to call another function subprogram. It is evident that FUN is a subprogram because it is not dimensioned in SUB1, as it would necessarily be if FUN were a subscripted variable. However, there is no clue there within SUB1 regarding just what function it is supposed to call. Now look back at the first CALL in the main program and you will see that a function name, SIN, is included in the argument list. Evidently SIN in the call is to be substituted for FUN in SUB1, so it will call in turn the well-known library, or **INTRINSIC** function SIN. The first statement in the main program thus makes sure that the third argument in the call will not be mistaken for an ordinary variable, and identifies the function SUB1 is to call as one of the available library functions. When SUB1 is to call a user subprogram, then the call from the main program must be preceded by the **EXTERNAL** designation. This is illustrated by the third CALL in the main program, and the subsequent call from SUB1 to the function SUM. Function SUM, of course is not among the available library (or intrinsic) functions and so is to be regarded as external for the purpose at hand. Note carefully, the INTRINSIC and EXTERNAL designations appear in the main program, not in a subprogram.

```
C
C TRIAL WITH INTRINSIC/EXTERNAL
C
      INTRINSIC SIN, COS
      EXTERNAL SUM
      DATA A,B,C /3*1.0/
      CALL SUB1 (X,A,SIN)
      PRINT*, X, A
      CALL SUB1 (Y,B,COS)
      PRINT*, Y, B
      CALL SUB1 (Z,C,SUM)
      PRINT*, Z, C
      END

      SUBROUTINE SUB1(W,D,FUN)
      W = FUN(D)
      RETURN
      END

      FUNCTION SUM(E)
      SUM = 5.0 + E
      RETURN
      END
```

3.12 COMMON

When you begin using subroutines regularly, you will find **COMMON** to be worthwhile. COMMON provides an alternative way to establish communication between a main program and its subprograms; it replaces part or all of the argument and parameter lists. As you will see, it also provides an alternative way to establish variables as being subscripted. A COMMON area is a section in a computer's memory set aside to hold values of variables that are shared between a main program and a subprogram, or between two or more subprograms. An exact description of the COMMON area must be included in each program or subprogram in which it is to be used. The essential description is provided by the COMMON statement. An example is:

```
COMMON L,X,Y(5),K(2)
```

This is a description of a common area in which the first location is to hold an integer and the second location a real. Locations 3 through 7 are the elements of a real array, 8 and 9 the elements of an integer array. In addition to providing space for two programs to share, this COMMON statement also serves to dimension the two arrays. To be of service, the same statement or one including the same type variables in the same sequence would be placed at the beginning of both the calling program and the subprogram. How about an example?

```
C
C SKELETON MAIN PROGRAM USING COMMON TO
C COMMUNICATE WITH A SUBROUTINE
C
      COMMON P,D,Q
      .
      CALL SOX
      .
      END
C
C SUBROUTINE ACCESSED VIA COMMON
C
      SUBROUTINE SOX
      COMMON R,S,T
      .
      RETURN
      END
```

In this example the pair of COMMON statements establishes communication between the main program and the subroutine. There is no list of arguments nor of parameters. The communication is established on the basis of the variables' positions in the COMMON statements. If, in the main program, a value is established for variable Q, the value is also available in the subroutine as the value of variable T. If, in the subprogram, the value of variable R is changed, the value available for variable P in the main program is changed the same way. When variables appear in COMMONs the variables' types must be consistent. If a variable in one COMMON statement is a

REAL variable, the variable corresponding to it in the other COMMON must also be REAL. You can include both REAL and INTEGER in the same COMMON, but don't try to include CHARACTER variables. Put all these in a COMMON of their own.

3.13 Subroutine Example

The following example includes several of the programming features that have been under recent discussion. Especially note the continuation of the X(J5) computation extending over four lines.

```
C
C SUBROUTINE SOLVER WILL SOLVE UP TO TEN
C EQUATIONS IN TEN UNKNOWNS
C
C N = NUMBER OF EQUATIONS
C P = ARRAY OF CONSTANT TERMS
C A = ARRAY OF COEFFICIENTS
C X = ARRAY OF SOLUTIONS
C
      SUBROUTINE SOLVER (N,P,A)
      COMMON X(10)
      DIMENSION P(10),A(10,10)
      NM1 = N - 1
      DO 4 I2=1,NM1
         J2 = I2+1
         DO 3 I3=J2,N
            CMULT=A(I3,I2)/A(I2,I2)
            P(I3)=P(I3)-P(I2)*CMULT
            DO 2 I4=I2,N
               A(I3,I4)=A(I3,I4)-A(I2,I4)*CMULT
2           CONTINUE
3        CONTINUE
4     CONTINUE
      DO 5 I5=1,N
         J5=N+1-I5
         X(J5)=(P(J5)-A(J5,1)*X(1)-A(J5,2)*X(2)
     1   -A(J5,3)*X(3)-A(J5,4)*X(4)-A(J5,5)*X(5)
     2   -A(J5,6)*X(6)-A(J5,7)*X(7)-A(J5,8)*X(8)
     3   -A(J5,9)*X(9)-A(J5,10)*X(10))/A(J5,J5)
5     CONTINUE
      RETURN
      END
```

This example subroutine promises solutions to systems of up to ten equations in ten unknowns. The principal variables are introduced in comments. The values needed for computation are transferred to the subroutine in the parameter list. The list includes an individual variable N and both a singly subscripted and a doubly subscripted array. The values determined for the equation variables are returned to the calling program in COMMON as the elements of the X array.

3.14 Labeled COMMON

Sometimes it seems as if the purveyors of Fortran have gone too far. If you began to feel this way in your encounter with subprograms and COMMON, you probably won't be too thrilled with this section. Fact is, the first time through you can skip over this section, especially if you resolve to use the same COMMON statement in a main program and in each of its subprograms. But sometimes this means transferring values to subprograms and then never using them there. By now you sense the unrest this sort of situation would create among the faithful; almost any Fortran zealot would soon resolve to find a better way. The better way this time is **labeled COMMON**.

In mild contrast to the current topic, the COMMON discussed previously is referred to as **unlabeled** (no surprise) or **blank** COMMON. A programmer using only the blank variety toils at some disadvantage in the next situation. Suppose you had the following in a main program:

```
COMMON A, B, C, D
```

And suppose further that in one subprogram you wanted to exchange values with only A and B, whereas in the other subprogram you needed to exchange with only C and D. True, this is not particularly momentous when the whole list includes only four variables, but remain attentive for a minute and get the point. The first subprogram presents no problem, we simply omit variables C and D from the subprogram's COMMON. Let's hope by now you realize that the situation isn't quite so simple in the second subprogram. For example, when used in the second subprogram:

```
COMMON C, D
```

just won't work, because the exchange is made on the basis of corresponding position. The first variable in the subroutine's COMMON would get the value from variable A in the main program. It makes no difference what variable name is used in the subprogram. In such situations labeling provides an improved way to go. The variables in the main program are grouped, and a name, or **label**, is attached to each group. As you will see in the following, the labels are enclosed in slashes, which is opposite the form used in DATA statements.

```
COMMON / SET1 / A, B
COMMON / SET2 / C, D
```

With this combination in the main program, the stage is set to use:

```
COMMON / SET2 / X, Y
```

in the second subprogram. Different variable names have been used here to remind us all about the independence in variable naming. Of course, variable X in the subprogram gets the value of variable C in the calling program. Note that the naming of labels is **not** independent. The same label must be used in the main program and the subprogram. Moreover, the number of variables in a labeled list must always be the same.

3.15 LOGICAL

The fourth of Fortran's four dominant data types is **logical.** All who have ventured to this point have had some experience with the type, even if their programming efforts haven't always been logical. As noted in an earlier section, the Fortran IF always introduces a question. In the form encountered thus far, the question is represented by one of the relational operators with a couple of variables or with a variable and a constant. For example, the statement:

```
IF(K .GT. 3) GO TO 55
```

raises the question: 'Is K greater than 3?' The answer to the question results in program control taking one or the other of two paths. Control either will be transferred to statement 55, or it will transfer to the next instruction following the IF. Consistent with this two-branch feature, the contents of the parens in the IF are capable of having one of only two possible values. In everyday discourse we could represent the two as on or off, zero or one, plus or minus, etc. In Fortran's logical domain the two values are designated as .TRUE. and .FALSE.; these are regarded as constants, the **only** logical constants. As these configurations appear in the body of a program, the decimal points are included. When a variable is declared to be LOGICAL, then .TRUE. or .FALSE. are the **only** values that can be assigned to it.

Logical type enables storing and manipulating answers to elementary questions and, as you will see, enables representing some involved questions. Consider the sequence:

```
C
C GETTING A HANDLE ON LOGICAL
C
      LOGICAL A, K
      .
      .
      A = .TRUE.
      K = (R .GT. S)
      .
```

This example starts by declaring variables A and K to be of the type we are considering. Note that variable names ordinarily real or integer can be used. There is no default typing of logical variables in the way A, B, C, . . ., H variables are regarded as REAL and I, J, . . ., N variables are regarded as INTEGER. Just as with CHARACTER type, LOGICAL must be declared.

The example shows the logical constant .TRUE. being assigned to variable A. We can't be sure of the value assigned to variable K because some program statements are not shown. If the value held by real variable R is greater than that held by S, the value .TRUE. will be assigned to K as well. Following these two assignments it would make sense to program either IF(K) GO TO 9 or IF (A) GO TO 4. Perhaps you sense that you have been using LOGICAL for some time, and you may be wondering why the fuss over matters that don't seem particularly exciting. The preamble here is intended to introduce Fortran's logical operators. These do their thing among logical variables and constants in a manner similar to the way relational operators perform with real and integer variables and constants. There are three logical operators:

```
.NOT.
.AND.
.OR.
```

The first one operates on individual logical variables. For instance, following the last example sequence, the operation part of a Fortran statement could reasonably include:

```
= .NOT. A
```

If you don't agree this should yield the value .FALSE. perhaps you should reread this section. Of course, it would be just as proper to program something like:

```
= .NOT. (R .GT. S)
```

and the results of either of these operations could be assigned to something, as long as the something is a logical variable.

The operators .AND. and .OR. do their operating with two logicals, or with the long-hand representations of the questions for which the logicals hold the answers. You said you wanted an example. Recalling that A and K have been declared LOGI-CAL and presuming that the others are more ordinary variables, it could make sense to program any of the following operations:

```
= A .AND. K
= A .OR. K
= K .AND. (P .LT. Q)
= (X .GT. Y) .OR. (M .LT. N)
```

As you no doubt divine, the first operation yields .TRUE. only when A and K are **both** true. The second yields .TRUE. when **either** A or K are .TRUE., and so on.

There are a couple of points to note in passing. If you need many logicals, you will be pleased to learn that logical arrays are practical. You can also provide for input and output of logical values with free-format READ* and PRINT*. Of course, you suspect by now that another FORMAT is lurking in the wings, probably you also suspect that it is L-type. If you have developed facility in using I-type and A-type, the new one should present no problems. However, it is remarkably insensitive to characters other than Ts and Fs, so you may not find L-type too exciting.

3.16 Multiple-Consideration Decisions

Facility with LOGICAL operations inevitably leads to an urge to incorporate several relational considerations into a single decision. Situations arise in which this is a very great convenience, but until the situations arise, the convenience may not be particularly evident. Perhaps an example will help:

```
IF(A .GT. B .AND. R .LT. S .OR. M .NE. J) PRINT*,XYZ
```

This IF raises three questions, and all three must be resolved before the desired decision can be made. Notwithstanding the several considerations, observe that transfer will be made to one of only two alternatives. Either the value held by variable XYZ will be printed, or it won't.

If we were so inclined, the answers to the three questions could first be assigned to logical variables:

```
LOGICAL D,E,F,G
D = (A .GT. B)
E = (R .LT. S)
F = (M .NE. J)
G = (D .AND. E .OR. F)
IF (G) PRINT*,XYZ
```

Here the answer to the compound question is assigned to yet another logical variable, G. This enables the IF to appear refreshingly simple.

Other combinations of relational operators and ordinary variables, together with combinations of logical variables and operators, can be built up to represent some of the world's weightiest problems. In some instances, pairs of logical operators work effectively in tandem. For example, the combinations .AND..NOT. and .OR..NOT. are legal and may stimulate some programmers to conjure up situations in which they could be of service. If you get involved in this sort of thing, be aware that there is hierarchical order among the operators, just as there is among the arithmetic operations. Unless directed otherwise by parens, the logical operators are evaluated in the order: .NOT., .AND., and .OR.. When in doubt regarding the ordering, include parens to force the operations to be performed the way you intend.

3.17 Multiple-Alternative Decisions

In contrast to multiple-consideration decisions, which take one or the other of two branches, multiple-alternative decisions can lead to any one of a great many program paths. Although these situations could be programmed by a suitable number of separate IFs, a more effective means is to link a second IF to the ELSE branch of a preceding IF. The ELSE branch of the second IF leads in turn to a third IF and so on. The result is a cascade-like program structure that selects one of several possible courses of action. Here, if the selection is to be made correctly, the governing conditions must be tested in prescribed order. The next example includes such a series of tests.

The principal feature of the current example is the decision block beginning with the first IF. Note that the decision points are considered in order from high to low. If a student qualifies for the first group, the student's report is produced, including the first message. If the student does not qualify, the ELSE branch leads to the next IF and the second test is made. Program control leaves the block after any report is produced, so only one report is produced for each student. In the form shown, the ELSE and following IF appear on the same line. If the following IF were on a different program line, then multiple ENDIFs would be required, and restricting the output to only one report per student would not be so simple.

```
C
C SUBROUTINE TO PRODUCE END-OF-TERM STUDENT REPORTS
C EACH INCLUDING ONE OF FOUR ASSESSMENT STATEMENTS
C BASED ON THE VALUE OF A COMPOSITE SCORE, COMSCR
C
      SUBROUTINE SELECT (NAME1,NAME2,COMSCR)
      CHARACTER *10 NAME1,NAME2
      PRINT 100, NAME1,NAME2
C
C MULTIPLE-ALTERNATIVE DECISION BLOCK
C
      IF (COMSCR .GE. 850.0) THEN
         PRINT 101, NAME1
      ELSE IF (COMSCR .GE. 700.0) THEN
         PRINT 102, NAME1
      ELSE IF (COMSCR .GE. 600.0) THEN
         PRINT 103, NAME1
      ELSE
         PRINT 104, NAME1
      ENDIF
      RETURN
  100 FORMAT (' TERM REPORT FOR' ,2A10,/)
  101 FORMAT (1X ,A10,', YOUR TERM GRADE IS A')
  102 FORMAT (1X ,A10,', YOUR TERM GRADE IS B')
  103 FORMAT (1X ,A10,', YOUR TERM GRADE IS C')
  104 FORMAT (1X ,A10,', YOU ARE SCHEDULED FOR A RETEST',/,
     1 12X,'AT 2PM ON DECEMBER 25')
      END
```

3.18 Multiple Subscripts

A word of explanation seems justified regarding withholding consideration of multiple subscripts until along about now. Why, you may have wondered, not consider single, double, and then higher-order subscripted arrays in direct sequence? Well, the hope in establishing the order followed here is that fledgling programmers will have made substantial use of single subscripts before they undertake encounter with double subscripts. If this were some sort of ideal world, then one would entertain consideration of double subscripts only after a accumulated experience with one-dimension arrays had shown them to be inadequate, or sufficiently inconvenient for a prospective task, to justify developing skill with sets of two dimensions. Corresponding experience with two-dimension arrays would then precede moving on to consider larger sets of subscripts. Truly, you are not going to have time and energy to learn about everything, and if double subscripts serve your purposes adequately, your best course at this point may be to skip the present section. But if you remain involved with programming, the need may arise to deal with an unwieldy number of doubly-subscripted variables or two-dimension arrays. When and if this happens to you, consider using subscripts of order higher than two. Chances are that your Fortran will handle subscripts high enough, or deep enough to serve your most demanding purpose. If you have first mastered single subscripts, then made the transition from single to double subscripts without undue toil, then you are as ready as you will ever be to experience the convenience and the frustration of using multiple subscripts.

The words **high** and **deep** in the last paragraph refer to the levels of subscripting, not the size of individual subscripts. A variable that is to be subscripted four deep could be introduced with:

```
DIMENSION AB(6,5,3,2)
```

This statement reserves 180 locations for a variable named AB. The geometric approach may help here. Think first of a two-dimension variable with 6 rows and 5 columns. Next visualize three of these 6 by 5s placed side by side to form a rectangular parallelopiped with dimensions 6x5x3. Now think of two of these parallelopipeds side by side; taken together they represent the variable AB. Frequently the application will suggest names for the levels of subscripts. In the present instance consider identifiers **row, column, slice** and **box.** Array AB thus consists of six rows, five columns, three slices and two boxes.

We can use any of the array elements as we would an ordinary program variable, for example by reading into AB(1,5,2,1), or by adding the contents of AB(1,1,3,1) to the contents of AB(1,2,3,1) and assigning the sum to AB(1,3,3,1). Suitable values could be read into the whole array with:

```
READ*, AB
```

But remember sufficient data must be provided to fill all 180 elements. Too, observe that the first column in the first 6x5 in the first parallelopiped will be filled before the second column. Let's hope you agree that the first 6x5 slice will be filled before any values are read into the second slice, and that the first box will be filled before any values find their way into the second box. Reading into the array in a different order requires program control of the subscripts. For example, data values could be read into the middle 6x5 slice in the second box, filling in a row at a time with the following:

```
      DO 10 IR=1,6
        READ 101, (AB(IR,IC,2,2),IC=1,5)
10    CONTINUE
```

If the aforegoing has piqued your curiosity, why not try programming with an array that is dimensioned three or more deep. Keep the several dimensions small at first and check intermediate results by frequent printing. Try reading data into a 5x4x3 'box,' then print out the values that would be in your view when looking at the box from the right side. Chances are that related skills will develop faster by such exercising than they will as a result of reading about them.

3.19 DOUBLE PRECISION

Most humans are favorably impressed when they learn that the computer can keep track of seven or eight significant figures. They probably would never even think of situations in which more precision would be necessary or even desirable. After all, when buying fence for a circular garden it doesn't help much to know that the numerals 65358979 can be tacked on to 3.141592 to get a more precise estimate of the ratio between the circumference and the diameter of a circle. Experience with similar practical situations may prompt disregard for Fortran's capacity for extending the number of significant digits carried along in computation. This is unfortunate because DOUBLE PRECISION is a very handy capability in some situations.

To use double precision, a type declaration first tells the compiler the names of all the variables that are to enjoy this exalted status. Next, the programmer must bolster all constants that are to enter the calculations because the precision of the results will be limited to that of the least precise factor. DOUBLE PRECISION constants are identified by a trailing D, with two numerals indicating the powers of ten to be included. For example, 3.500000000000000 would as well be entered as 0.35D01. This is more than a convenience. If the D-factor is not present, only the first eight or so digits are considered, even though a constant may include as many as 15 apparently significant zeros. There is no provision for changing type from DOUBLE PRECISION to REAL, or otherwise. Some compilers issue a caution if a careless programmer includes two types in an operation or attempts to assign a REAL constant to a D-P variable. Others don't. Your best bet is, if you elect to use the new type, take care to be consistent throughout.

Evidently list-directed input and output of DOUBLE PRECISION values is compiler-dependent. When using free-format, one compiler at hand directs reading and printing of 15 or more digits, another yields only nine. Perhaps you have begun to suspect that one more FORMAT will be needed if full advantage of the new type is to be realized. To no one's surprise, the FORMAT this time is D-type. In form and function it is similar to F- and E-type, but the numbers are usually larger. The example that follows may serve to get you started with DOUBLE PRECISION. For many it will be more than enough.

```
C
C DOUBLE PRECISION EXAMPLE
C
      DOUBLE PRECISION R,P,C
      R = 0.35D+03
      P = 3.141592653589793D00
      C = R*P
      PRINT 101, R,P,C
  101 FORMAT(1X,D25.15)
      END
```

If you become involved with DOUBLE PRECISION, you will be glad to learn that several library functions are generally available. In several instances the function names are the same as before, but with a D prefix. The names DABS, DEXP, DSIN, and DSQRT are indicative of the dozen or so functions ready to serve you.

3.20 COMPLEX

A popular means for representing and manipulating vector quantities is to first reduce or resolve them into components. In some situations the two components are interpreted to be the same in nature, but directed in different ways. For instance, an oblique velocity is resolved into a horizontal and a vertical component. But each component is still regarded as a velocity. In other situations the two components are regarded as different in their natural form. Complex numbers are used in such situations. Here the distinction is made between a real and an imaginary part. The real part of the complex number is the one we feel at ease with. In geometric representation we usually think of it as similar to the vector component that represents horizontal velocity. The other part of the complex number seems strange. It is strange. It is associated with that troublesome character *i*, the square root of negative one. It is so strange we call it imaginary. How strange can something get?

Fortran isn't particularly bothered by the way we chose to interpret the two parts carried along by variables declared to be COMPLEX. The essential feature is that there are two parts. Whenever reading into or printing the value of a COMPLEX variable, provision must be made to accommodate two quantities. The same is necessary when assigning values, as shown in the next example:

```
C
C COMPLEX-TYPE EXAMPLE
C
      COMPLEX P,D,Q,R,S,T
      P = (3.0,4.0)
      D = (-2.0,2.0)
      Q   P+D
      R = P-D
      S = P*D
      T = P/D
      PRINT*, P,D,Q
      PRINT*, R,S,T
      END
```

The example starts off by declaring six variables to be of the type being considered. Next, two-part constants are assigned to variables P and Q. Observe that the assigned values are REAL constants enclosed in parens. The parens make sure that the two parts of a COMPLEX constant stay together. Four familiar operations follow, this time performed with the new type variables. Addition and subtraction of P and Q are straightforward. If you think of velocities or displacements while contemplating the arithmetic, the results will represent velocities or displacements. If you are thinking of vectors in a real-imaginary plane, the results probably will represent vectors in a real-imaginary plane. Either way the result from the addition will be (1.0,6.0), and the subtraction will yield (5.0,2.0). A bit more effort may be needed to check the results of the P*D and P/D, which are (-14.0,-2.0) and (0.25,-1.75) respectively. If you haven't encountered real-world situations that can be represented by such gyrations, all this may not be too exciting, but the time may come when you regard this last of Fortran's data types as a real blessing.

Standard Fortran includes a couple of library functions which serve programmers who venture into the world of COMPLEX. The first, fittingly named **CMPLX**, puts two REAL quantities together and readies them for further operations in which they will be the two components of a complex quantity. Be sure to assign the results from CMPLX only to a variable that has been suitably declared.

Two other functions work the other way around. They take apart a COMPLEX, returning either the real or the imaginary (the first one or the second) component. It is unfortunate that the first of these two functions was named **REAL**. Try to keep this REAL separate from the type declaration having the same name, **and** from the other function that has the same name but operates on solitary integers. The present REAL operates on something that is COMPLEX, and, as you have no doubt guessed by now, sends back the first of the two parts. The other part, the one customarily associated with the imaginary component, is produced by the function **AIMAG**. The present REAL and AIMAG can be regarded as REAL-type functions that operate on COMPLEX arguments, CMPLX as a COMPLEX function that works on two variable arguments that have been declared REAL-type.

Most Fortrans permit multiplication of COMPLEX variables by REAL-type constants and variables, even by integers, as well as some mixed-type addition and subtraction. As you probably suspect, when you add or subtract a constant, it is figured in with the first of the two components. Exponentiation of complex quantities is permitted, although only with INTEGER exponents. Furthermore, COMPLEX quantities can be passed to subroutines, either in an argument-parameter list combination or in COMMON. If you try this, remember to declare and COMMON all variables involved in the transfer, both in the main program and in the subroutine.

COMPLEX input and output can be processed with list-directed READ* and PRINT* instructions. When reading values in this way, be sure to include each pair within a set of parens. This is similar to reading in CHARACTER constants that must be enclosed in quotes. List-directed printing of COMPLEX quantities will appear as ordered pairs enclosed in parens. If formatted input or output is desired, F-type serves very well. Of course, two fields are involved. When reading in with FORMAT control, forget the parens—well, just don't include them in the data. And don't look for them in formatted output.

If all this regarding COMPLEX seems depressingly complex, look at the bright side; COMPLEX is the first of Fortran's data types that has not prompted the need for yet another FORMAT.

3.21 Programmed File Management

All who have ventured this far have necessarily been involved in the business of file management. The management has consisted principally of creating, changing, saving, and retrieving the files that serve as vehicles for programs and data. Usually the operating system does part of the managing, the part depending on the age and the sophistication of the system. For instance, contemporary editors automatically save increments of files as they are created, thus preventing inadvertent loss. On older and simpler systems, such loss of a file remains a distinct possibility. The system also assists in transmitting program and data files for processing, again in its own way. On one of three systems at hand, the program file and the data file are submitted separately in sequence. This corresponds to operations with punched cards, in which a program deck and a data deck were read in sequence into a card reader. On another system the program file and data file are combined with the help of an editor, and the combined file is submitted. The program is compiled and then executed; the system assures that the data are right there when needed at execution time. The third system does the compilation, producing a file of machine-language instructions; execution is directed by human intervention and the person must provide any data needed. Each of the foregoing could be said to use standard input and output; the input provided through the terminal keyboard or by files in sequence and the output going to the terminal screen or a line printer.

Standard input/output is ineffective when large amounts of information must be preserved for subsequent processing. It doesn't take much imagination to see why this is so. Suppose the volume of output from a current program practically fills a computer's memory, say, output equivalent in volume to the current edition of the telephone directory for a large city. Of course, the information will be needed for updating and printing next year's directory, but standard input/output leave us with an unfortunate choice. One choice would be to leave the information in the computer's memory, perhaps entering changes from time to time. This would work, of course, but it would be expensive, and maintaining pleasant relations with other potential users might present a problem. The other choice would be to run off a copy of this year's directory on the line printer and release the computer's memory to serve other users. But now, before the information can be updated and the next edition printed, someone has to sit at a terminal and enter all the information, an assignment we all agree is not particularly enchanting.

Relief from this unfortunate state of affairs is available through the use of **external** or **auxiliary** storage. A computer's capacity imposes no limit on the amount of auxiliary storage used. The stored information resides on a magnetic disk or tape similar to that used in audio cassettes. By now you must suspect that Fortran supports the use of auxiliary storage. Fortran enables us to program the creation of files and the retrieval of information from files existing on auxiliary storage. The capacity here is in addition to that provided by a system. Even a simple system will have a **save** capability. Here the system transmits the saved file to auxiliary storage. In some contrast, the feature to be considered next is the transmission of information to, and retrieval from, auxiliary storage by **program** control. Whether we use program control or system control to manage files depends on the person's preference, the system capability, and the circumstances.

Contemporary Fortran enables use of two types of files: **direct access** and **sequential.** Both types can contain any practical number of records. Records are groups of data items that belong together. For example, a record in a bank's file could consist of a customer's name, address, account number, number of deposits and withdrawals, current account balance, etc. All these data items are processed together. In particular, information transmitted to and stored in files is processed in records. When records are small, they can be regarded as corresponding to lines in a file as created with an editor. Of course, a record in an auxiliary storage file could hold the information from many lines in a file as created with an editor. The actual form in which the information is stored on disk or tape is referred to as the **physical record**. Those of us using Fortran don't have to worry about physical records; the compiler handles these details. We must, however, select between formatted and unformatted records. Information in unformatted records exists in the same form used within a computer's memory. This expedites rapid storing and retrieval of large files but precludes human interpretation, unless the human is addicted to long strings of ones and zeros. Accordingly, only formatted records are considered in the examples to follow.

A word of counsel seems in order regarding initial efforts to program file management. As most of you realize by now, differences in operating systems and compilers can make things that work in one place not work in another. The fact that the following example programs worked in one environment does not ensure that they will run effectively in any other place. The moral here is: Do not become discouraged. The ability to write into and read from files represents a substantial extension of programming skill. In addition to advancing programming skill, efforts probably will test your frustration tolerance.

3.22 Direct Access Files

When using the direct access file option, the programmer can write into and read from any record in a file. Because this is usually desirable, direct access is featured here in the first examples. However, direct access is available only on systems having disk storage. And some systems having disk storage will not support direct accessing of records. Many readers are familiar with the operation of home-based computers with floppy disk storage. When several files have been stored, the system provides direct access to individual files but not to records within files.

As evident in the present example, the stage is set for programming file manipulation with the OPEN instruction. This instruction allows information to be transferred by establishing a unit number and a file name. In general, the programmer selects the unit number, although the system may reserve some numbers. The file name is entered as a character string, within single quotes. Together, the unit number and the file name establish the place to which the information is to go and from which it can subsequently be retrieved. Other entries in the OPEN statement establish the means of access, the form, and the status. As shown, the key entries are entered as character strings. In the present instance, inasmuch as the file is being created, it is properly designated as a new file. The final item in the OPEN statement establishes the length of all records to be stored in the file. In direct access files, all records have the same length. In the present instance, each record is to be 30 characters in length; note carefully the agreement with this and the total field length specified by the FORMAT in statement 101.

```
C
C     PROGRAM TO CREATE A DIRECT ACCESS FILE
C
C THE PROGRAM READS IN THE NAME OF A TEAM AND A WEEK'S
C SUM OF AT BATS AND HITS. THE INFORMATION IS TRANSMITTED
C TO THE FILE WITH A WRITE, NOT A PRINT.
C
C
      CHARACTER *10 TM
      INTEGER BATS, HITS
C
C DESIGNATE UNIT AND FILE NAME, ETC.
C
      OPEN(UNIT=3, FILE-'TEAM', ACCESS='DIRECT',
     2     FORM='FORMATTED', STATUS='NEW', RECL=30)
      DO 10 IR=1,10
C
C READ DATA FROM STANDARD INPUT
C
        READ 101, TM, BATS, HITS
C
C WRITE TO UNIT3 AS DESIGNATED
C
        WRITE(UNIT=3, FMT=101, REC=IR) TM, BATS, HITS
   10 CONTINUE
  101 FORMAT(A10,2I10)
C
C CLOSE THE FILE ON UNIT 3
C
      CLOSE(UNIT=3, STATUS='KEEP')
      STOP
      END
```

The example program reads from standard input first within the DO 10 loop. Next, the information is written, not printed, in the file. The WRITE instruction refers to the unit identified in the OPEN statement and includes the statement number of the controlling FORMAT in a new form, that is, FMT=101. Finally, the WRITE includes the identifier for each record written. In direct access files, each record has its own identifier or **record number**. The record numbers are established when the records are first written. Subsequent reference to individual records is established by these record numbers. In the present example, the current value of the loop index is used to establish each record number. For example, when using standard input data in the form:

```
        1         2         3         4
1234567890123456789012345678901234567890

GOPHERS        145       23
GREMLINS       154       18
CHIPMUNKS      161       33
     .          .         .
```

GREMLINS, etc. is written into the second record in file TEAM. The CLOSE statement signals the end of programmed file manipulations. Here the unit is confirmed, and, in at least one system, the concluding status is designated. At the conclusion of the run, the file TEAM resides in the appropriate file space.

The next example reads from both standard input and from the file created by the last example program. Inasmuch as the file TEAM has been previously created, the proper status is now OLD.

```
C
C THIS PROGRAM READS EACH TEAM'S NAME TOGETHER WITH THE CURRENT
C WEEK'S TOTAL AT BATS AND HITS FROM STANDARD INPUT. THE PROGRAM
C NEXT READS THE CUMULATIVE AT BATS AND HITS FROM THE FILE 'TEAM' ON
C UNIT 3. THE DATA ARE COMBINED AND THE CURRENT AVERAGES COMPUTED.
C THE TEAM NAMES AND CURRENT TOTALS ARE PRINTED VIA STANDARD
C OUTPUT, TOGETHER WITH THE CURRENT TEAM AVERAGES. THE UPDATED
C COUNTS ARE THEN WRITTEN TO THE FILE ON UNIT 3.
C
      CHARACTER*10 TM,TX
      INTEGER BATS, HITS, BATX, HITX
      REAL AVE
C
C OPEN THE FILE, NOTE IT IS AN OLD FILE NOW
C
      OPEN(UNIT=3, FILE='TEAM', ACCESS='DIRECT'
    2     FORM='FORMATTED', STATUS='OLD', RECL=30)
      DO 10 IR=1,10
C
C READ FIRST FROM STANDARD INPUT, THEN FROM FILE 'TEAM'
C
         READ 101, TM, BATS, HITS
         READ (UNIT=3, FMT=101, END=99, REC=IR) TX, BATX, HITX
         IF (TM .NE. TX) THEN
            PRINT*,' TEAM MISMATCH', IR, TM, TX
            STOP
  500    ENDIF
         BATS = BATS + BATX
         HITS = HITS + HITX
         AVE = REAL(HITS)/REAL(BATS)
C
C PRINT OUT THE UPDATED TOTALS AND THE AVERAGES, THEN
C WRITE THE UPDATED TOTALS TO THE FILE
C
         PRINT 102, TM, BATS, HITS, AVE
         WRITE(UNIT=3, FMT=101, REC=IR) TM, BATS, HITS
   10 CONTINUE
  101 FORMAT(A10,2I10)
  102 FORMAT(' ',A10,' BATS',I4,' HITS',I4,' AVE',F6.3)
      CLOSE(UNIT=3, STATUS='KEEP')
   99 PRINT*,' FOUND END OF FILE'
      STOP
      END
```

Other items in the OPEN statement are the same as in the earlier example. Within the DO 10 loop, reading is again done first from standard input. Next, a record is read from the file. Observe the provision against reading through the end of the file provided by the END=99. Protection against entering a wrong team's current data or entering a team's data in the wrong record in the file is provided by the block IF. The statement number 500 doesn't contribute to the operation of the program, but without it the compiler objects because no transfer is possible to an unnumbered statement following a STOP.

After reading from standard input and the file, the present example updates the at bats and hits and computes the current team average. All this is printed out on standard output, then the updated at bats and hits are written in the file. The operation here may not seem so different from that in the next example set, but in the present scheme each individual record can be accessed. If the DO and CONTINUE instructions were removed and the record number were set to an appropriate integer in the WRITE instruction, for example, REC=3, only that record would be accessed.

3.23 Sequential Access Files

In comparison with the last example set, the principal difference to be noted is the substitution of SEQUENTIAL for DIRECT in the access designation. A minor difference is the optional way of entering the unit number in the OPEN statement.

```
C
C    PROGRAM TO CREATE A SEQUENTIAL FILE
C
C THIS PROGRAM READS TEAM NAMES AND A WEEK'S PRODUCTION INTO
C SUITABLE ARRAYS. THE READING IS DONE FROM STANDARD INPUT.
C WRITING TO THE FILE IS DONE FROM THE ARRAYS.
C
      CHARACTER*10 TM(10)
      INTEGER BATS(10) , HITS(10)
      OPEN(1,FILE='TEAM1' , ACCESS 'SEQUENTIAL',
     2      STATUS='NEW', FORM='FORMATTED')
C
C READ TEAM NAME, BATS, AND HITS FROM STANDARD INPUT
C
      DO 10 IR=1,10
         READ 101, TM(IR), BATS(IR), HITS(IR)
   10 CONTINUE
C
C WRITE THE ARRAY CONTENTS TO THE FILE
C
      DO 20 IR=1,10
         WRITE(1,FMT=101) TM(IR), BATS(IR), HITS(IR)
   20 CONTINUE
  101 FORMAT(A10,2I10)
      CLOSE(UNIT=1,STATUS='KEEP')
   99 STOP
      END
```

In the form shown here, the number appearing first is interpreted the same as UNIT=1 would be. No record length is designated when opening sequential files; it is possible for successive records to be of different lengths. The big point here is that, once begun, the writing to the file continues to the end. A given record cannot be accessed without first accessing all the previous records in the file.

The final example in the current series illustrates the updating of a sequential file.

```
C
C EXAMPLE PROGRAM TO UPDATE A SEQUENTIAL FILE
C
      CHARACTER*10 TM(10), TX(10)
      INTEGER BATS(10), HITS(10), BATX(10), HITX(10)
      REAL AVE(10)
      OPEN(1, FILE='TEAM1', ACCESS='SEQUENTIAL',
     2      FORM='FORMATTED', STATUS='OLD')
C
C READ NEW INFORMATION FROM STANDARD INPUT
C
      DO 10 IR=1,10
          READ 101, TM(IR), BATS(IR), HITS(IR)
   10 CONTINUE
C
C REWIND THE SEQUENTIAL FILE BEFORE READING
C THEN READ THE OLD TOTALS FROM THE FILE
C
      REWIND(1)
      DO 20 IR=1,10
          READ(1,FMT=101,END=99) TX(IR), BATX(IR), HITX(IR)
   20 CONTINUE
C
C UPDATE THE TOTALS AND COMPUTE CURRENT AVERAGES
C
      DO 30 IR=1,10
          HITS(IR)=HITS(IR)+HITX(IR)
          BATS(IR)=BATS(IR)+BATX(IR)
          AVE(IR)=REAL(HITS(IR))/REAL(BATS(IR))
   30 CONTINUE
C
C REWIND THE FILE, PRINT OUT THE CURRENT TOTALS AND
C AVERAGES, THEN WRITE UPDATED TOTALS IN THE FILE
C
      REWIND(1)
      DO 40 IR=1,10
          PRINT 102, TM(IR), BATS(IR), HITS(IR), AVE(IR)
          WRITE(1, FMT=101) TM(IR), BATS(IR), HITS(IR)
   40 CONTINUE
  101 FORMAT(A10,2I10)
  102 FORMAT(A10,' BATS' ,I4,' HITS' ,I4,' AVE' ,F6.3)
      CLOSE(1,STATUS='KEEP')
   99 PRINT*, 'END OF FILE FOUND'
      STOP
```

Again, a current week's output of at bats and hits is read from standard input. Next, the cumulative totals are read from the file; both the current week's output and the cumulative totals are stored in suitable arrays. The DO 30 loop updates the counts of at bats and hits and computes the current team averages. Then the DO 40 loop prints out the current summary and writes the updated counts to the file.

The REWIND instruction demonstrates a principal difference between sequential and direct access files. Inasmuch as sequential files are processed from beginning to end, an existing file must usually be positioned at the beginning before either writing or reading. Such positioning is the function of REWIND. In the event that the file is already positioned at its beginning, REWIND has no effect.

3.24 File Management Exercises

1. Program the creation of a direct access file on your system. Determine the form of the file created. Try reading from the file as if it were in different form.

2. Program the creation of a sequential file. Check the form of this file, and then prepare a program to update the file. Check the effect of omitting any REWIND instructions.

3.25 Implicit Type Declaration

As noted in earlier sections, the data type for any variable can be established as the programmer wishes with a type declaration statement. The declaration is optional when using Fortran's REAL and INTEGER, but it must be used for any other type. The declaration can be made more general through the use of the IMPLICIT statement in the declaration. For example, the statement:

```
IMPLICIT INTEGER (A, B, D - G)
```

designates the type for all variables beginning with the letters A and B, and for variables beginning with the letters from D to G, inclusive. The same procedure can be followed with any of the other types as long as the IMPLICIT declaration appears before other declaration statements and before any executable statements.

Following the example IMPLICIT declaration, we can still specify an individual variable as desired, either confirming or overriding the previous declaration. For example:

```
REAL BOX, DOG
INTEGER ABX
```

Here the type for BOX and DOG has been explicitly declared, overriding the IMPLICIT specification. The explicit declaration for ABX simply confirms the previously established type.

Some enthusiasts contend that IMPLICIT typing has value for those seeking structure in their programs. For instance, one reviewer advocates beginning each program and subprogram with the statement:

```
IMPLICIT LOGICAL (A - Z)
```

and then overriding this with an explicit declaration for each variable used. This controls Fortran's easy acceptance of new variable names in obscure places within a program and makes sure that each variable name is up front, unless it happens to be a LOGICAL variable.

3.26 PARAMETER

Fortran's PARAMETER statement is used to establish a symbolic name for a constant. Of course, this can be done with an ordinary assignment statement, but the new way prevents subsequent change in the established value. The statement:

```
PARAMETER (PI = 3.14159, RHO = 0.0023245)
```

obviously establishes the designated values for variables PI and RHO. What isn't so obvious is that the established values can't be changed later on in the program. The variables can be used as many times as needed in the operation part of an instruction, but an attempt to assign a new value is doomed from the start.

3.27 Looping Operations III

In comparison with Fortran DOs of yore, those provided by contemporary compilers are amazingly cooperative. Present practice permits either INTEGERs or REALs to be used as control variables. The control variables can initiate with, or be decremented to, negative values and, when using a REAL control variable, can be incremented by decimal fraction amounts. Only integers were permitted to serve as controllers for DO loops in earlier versions of Fortran. Moreover, the control variable could only assume increasing values; the increment of change was always a positive integer. Perhaps you are working with an earlier Fortran version, so some of this section may not be as helpful as intended. Alternative procedures are noted for achieving the same results with dated facilities.

Two examples serve to illustrate the extended capability of contemporary DOs.

```
C
C EXAMPLE DO WITH DECREMENTED LOOP INDEX
C
      INTEGER SUM, M, N
      SUM = 0
      DO 60 M = 10,2,-2
        N=M
        SUM = SUM + N*N
  60  CONTINUE
      PRINT 101, SUM
      STOP
 101  FORMAT(1X,'THE DESIRED SUM IS:', I6,/)
      END
```

This loop forms the sum of squares of even numbers from 10 down to 2. Though we can't think of any particular instance in which we would want the desired sum, running the program should confirm something about your Fortran. If this won't work for you, of course, you could form the sum of squares of the even numbers from 2 up to

10. But if you really need the descending sequence of evens, just initialize another integer variable to 12 before entering the loop. Inside the loop, before doing anything else, decrement your new variable by two. In comparison with the new way, this is undeniably clumsy, but it works.

The second example introduces a REAL loop index, this one incremented by 0.1 each iteration. This little program generates a continued product, for which the significance and need remain obscure. But the control of the loop is straightforward enough. The REAL loop index is to start at 1.0 and advance to 4.0 in 0.1 unit increments. If it is your lot to toil without this capability, you will just have to run an integer loop index from 1 up to 40. Initialize a real variable to 0.9 before entering the loop, and increment the variable suitably each time around the loop.

```
C
C          HOW DO YOU DO NEW DO?
C EXAMPLE ILLUSTRATING REAL LOOP CONTROL
C     WITH DECIMAL FRACTION INCREMENTS
C
      B = 1.0
      DO 50 A = 1.0 ,4.0,0.1
         C = A
         B = B*C
         PRINT*, C,B
   50 CONTINUE
      END
```

The current example may serve to illustrate the accumulation of error that sometimes plagues looping. In satisfying the directed execution of the loop, one Fortran at hand arrived at the value of 3.99999833 for variable C. True, the percentage of evident error is not great, but then the loop hasn't been traversed many times. How far from the expected value would the sum be if 0.1 were added on 1,000 or 10,000 times? This depends on the size of the word used in the machine language of the computer doing the job.

3.28 Computed GO TO

An alternative way for programming multiple-alternative situations is the **computed GO TO**. When using this instruction, the value of an integer determines which of several transfers is to be made. Each branch is represented by a statement number, and all the statement numbers appear within a set of parens appearing just after the GO TO. The example statement is made to order for a six-alternative situation.

```
C
C COMPUTED GO TO
C
      GO TO (10,20,30,40,50,60),K
```

Here transfer is made to the statement number in the position corresponding to the value of K. If the value of K is 1, transfer goes to the first of the statement numbers appearing within the parens; if K is 2 transfer is to the second, and so on. As you can see, a suitable value must be established for the controlling integer before the GO TO can operate. The value must be greater than zero and no greater than the count of statement numbers within the parens. If the value of K were less than 1 or greater than 6, the statement following the computed GO TO would be executed. The computed GO TO is a compact instruction, but it requires transfer to remote places for getting things done. Contemporary practice regards such transfers unfavorably because the resulting programs are difficult for people to interpret.

3.29 EQUIVALENCE

When several individuals become involved in joint programming efforts, there is the chance that one person's naming or use of a variable will differ from that of another person. A similar situation can arise in the efforts of an individual who inadvertently uses two names for the same thing in a program. This is quite possible when preparing a long program unless you divide it into subprograms. In principle this sort of thing couldn't happen if you were using a more demanding language, one that required declaration of all variables. But Fortran is forgiving; it admits inadvertent introduction of new variable names. Probably that is why we have EQUIVALENCE. The Fortran statement:

```
EQUIVALENCE (T,W,F),(M,N)
```

would serve in a program in which variables T, W, and F had inadvertently been used for the same thing. Presumably this could result from a programmer's dawn-busting efforts on Tuesday, Wednesday, and Friday. Evidently the programmer used the first letter of the day for a key variable, having forgotten on Wednesday and Friday that it had already been named. We may be confident of the happy ending here; the example EQUIVALENCE inserted early in the program results in variables T, W, and F all being stored in the same location. As a result, they are all treated as the same variable. If the value of one is changed, all three have the new value.

As shown in the example, other variable sets can be made equivalent in the same EQUIVALENCE. Subscripted variables can also be included. Only one element of each array need be linked together. The rest of the elements fall in line. For example, the pair of statements:

```
C
C EQUIVALENCE WITH SUBSCRIPTED VARIABLES
C
      DIMENSION A(8),Z(3)
      EQUIVALENCE (A(6),Z(1))
```

first establish A and Z as subscripted, and then link the first element of Z to the sixth of A. Pursuant to this, Z(2) and A(7) will be treated as the same variable, as will Z(3) and A(8). No doubt you sense the impropriety of trying to EQUIVALENCE A(7) and Z(1). This would result in the Z array effectively sticking out through the bottom of the A array; surely disappointment would follow. When used sparingly, EQUIVALENCE can be a help, but excessive use makes programs difficult to interpret and probably signals potential advantage in the further use of subprograms.

3.30 Summary for Level Three

Programmers who have attained a third skill level will use double subscripts with ease and confidence; they will establish dimensions in any of three ways and be looking for a suitable application for triple subscripts. To the extent that support is available, their programs will make near-optimum use of looping. Level-three programmers will use subprograms, especially subroutines, with enthusiasm; programmed exchanges between main and subprograms will use any of three means. They will program multiple-consideration and multiple-alternative decision structures compactly and will have used either DOUBLE PRECISION or COMPLEX advantageously. The level of skill envisioned will usually be confirmed through regular use of files under program control.

Chapter 4

Delayed Preliminaries

A course comes to a beginning instead of an end. —M. I. Rasey[1]

As many readers know, the first thing doesn't always come in the beginning in the learning business. The second law of thermodynamics, for example, was established before the first. And, thereafter, more than 100 years passed until another law was recognized, one that was then seen to be a precursor to the other two. Designation of the new discovery as the zeroth law shows that practitioners of the day recognized the new law as one that would more properly have come first. In a similar vein, the items presented in this section could have been designated level zero. Here will be found matters that might more properly have been attended to at the beginning. Many will sense that program planning, for example, deserves consideration quite before the coding of program instructions. But in the practice of instruction, until a modicum of programming ability is in hand, program planning can be a sterile exercise. Thus, the route taken has led directly to the introduction of blocks of skills and the early practice in their use without much regard for the big picture into which the blocks are intended to fit. The approach attempted may be regarded similar to a **conversational** approach to the learning of a computer language. For many of us the learning of a computer language proceeds along lines similar to those followed in the learning of our native language. We start by becoming acquainted with bits and pieces, such as 'assignment' and 'PRINT*'; these correspond to the words and phrases we learn first in our native language. The bits and pieces fit together to make statements, blocks,

---

1. Marie I. Rasey (1887–1957) received B.A., M.A., and Ph.D. degrees from the University of Michigan and a doctorate from the Institute of Individual Psychology in Vienna. Her teaching career spanned 50 years, beginning at Galesburg, Michigan, high school and concluding as professor of educational psychology at Wayne State University.

and loops in the computer language. As skill in using our native language develops the words and phrases are combined to make clauses, sentences, and paragraphs. Most of us find some time spent in such a **bottom-up** approach essential to effective learning. An assumption implicit in the present approach is that all learners will engage in the bottom-up approach, at least to some degree. The degree likely depends upon the learning style of the individual.

A discontinuity appears when one proceeds to the task of relating a significant story in a native language, or preparing a significant program with Fortran or another computer language. One does not write a prize-winning novel, for instance, by simply lining up phrases. When a significant story is to be told, some thought is necessarily devoted to the plot. But remember, by the time the plot is being considered, the author-to-be is well versed in manipulating words and phrases, at least if the development of the story is to proceed in a manner likely to be regarded as satisfactory. Correspondingly, one does not produce a significant computer program by simply hooking together blocks and loops. An essential feature in the preparation of any significant program is a plan. By first considering the plan we engage in a **top-down** approach, either to the writing of a novel or the production of a program. Although some bottom-up activity is seen as essential to most learning, the creation of significant works inevitably involves one in the top-down approach. Pursuant to all this, some consideration will now be directed toward planning.

4.1 Program Planning

The approach to programming advocated thus far has been to involve the neophyte in producing and running a program at the earliest possible moment. The intended result, a measure of early success, is to provide an experience base on which to build and some confidence to endure the trying times we all encounter. The approach serves the needs of many beginners, although it does present a hazard. You can get the impression that the preparation of programs is generally done this way, that is, by plunging right into the production of program instructions or code. In general, this is not the case. For all but the most elementary programs, planning is essential. Actually some planning is necessarily done even for trivial programs, and as program complexity increases, the need for planning increases.

To better appreciate the business of program planning, compare the preparation of a computer program with the erection of a building. If the structure to be built is small and simple, there will be scant need for extensive planning. No doubt many journeymen can build a shed or garage without detailed plans, though even they needed a plan the first time. The need for planning becomes evident when the project increases in size and complexity until the builder cannot keep all the details under adequate control. Computer programming is similar. Simple programming tasks can be pursued with minimal planning yet with reasonable probability of success. The probability of such success drops as program complexity increases, especially when the efforts of several programmers are required. Without adequate planning, momentous programming projects are undertaken at considerable risk.

A further similarity is evident in the relationship between the person who is to own a building and the one who is to build the building. It is not unusual for a prospective owner to have but limited knowledge of building details; yet a meeting of minds must be achieved before the project can be effectively pursued. Adequate communication must be established regarding the form and function of the building. Tools for expediting this communication are sketches, scale drawings, models, and building specifications. A similar situation exists when the person who wants to implement a computer application is not the one who will produce the program. Communication is needed to specify the program's purpose and to establish the form of information supplied and the form in which the results are to appear. Tools for these functions are flowcharts or other diagrams, pseudocode, and program documents.

The planning of a program begins with the designation of all information that is to be provided as input, and the specification of the desired output. Only after these matters have been agreed to can the planning proceed with reasonable chance of success. Once the source and form of the input and the destination and use of the output are determined, the gross purpose usually becomes evident. Consideration of the desired output may reveal inadequacies in the planned input. If so, the inadequacies must be remedied. After attending to these matters, the planning proceeds through successive resolution of gross purpose into components, and into lesser components.

4.2 Flowcharts

Flow diagrams or flowcharts represent the operations to be performed and the transfers of information between operations in a program. The flow of information is represented by directed lines. Different types of operations are represented by different geometric shapes. Several of these are shown in Figure 1, a flowchart that

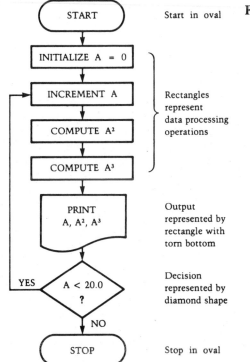

Start in oval

Rectangles represent data processing operations

Output represented by rectangle with torn bottom

Decision represented by diamond shape

Stop in oval

Figure 1. Flow diagram for Exercise 1.20.1

could serve for one of the early programming exercises. The beginning and the end of operations represented in a chart are ovals labeled **start** and **stop.** General data processing operations are shown as rectangles; decision points are represented by diamond shapes. Data input is customarily shown as a rectangle with a clipped corner (see Figure 2) and output as a rectangle with a torn bottom.

At one time the preparation of a comprehensive flowchart was held to be the *sine qua non*, an absolute prerequisite to any programming effort. If ever a neophyte were to seek aid for an errant program without first presenting a suitable flowchart, he or she would be unceremoniously rebuffed. In a great many instances, the diagram was indeed essential because the conventional programming of the time made such extensive use of the GO TO in one or another of its several forms. At the time (c. 1970) Fortran had been in existence for about 15 years. During this period the language had experienced brisk development and had become established as the high-level language for scientific and engineering data processing. Some inadequacies had been recognized, and, with the emergence of other computer languages, the shortcomings of Fortran began to receive increased attention. Much of the attention was focused on Fortran's GO TO. As we all realize by now, this enables transfer to remote program sections and leads to programs described as heavily interlocked and nonlocal. Hence, the then-conventional reliance on flow diagrams. With the introduction of further refinements in Fortran (for example, the block IF) and the increased use of subprograms, the need for the GO TO diminished. Now, in implementations that support a WHILE loop structure, there appears scant need for a GO TO. Indeed, some programmers have made a fetish of proscribing against this instruction that served us so long and faithfully. The ongoing eclipse of the GO TO has unquestionably influenced the flowchart's loss of popularity. As the GO TO has gone, the flowchart has lost its supremacy. It is included here because, for some programmers and for some circumstances, the flowchart can be a substantial aid. Later, we'll use a flowchart to show the details of a currently popular approach to program design.

4.3 Pseudocode

The representation of a program's function in the form of abbreviated statements in English is referred to as **pseudocode.** For some purposes this representation can be just as serviceable as a flow diagram. No knowledge of a programming language is needed to interpret pseudocode. If the abbreviation present in the pseudocode is not too severe, everyone who understands the English can follow the steps to be programmed. If sufficiently detailed, the pseudocode allows a program's function to be completely specified before any actual coding is done.

```
Pseudocode for finding square roots:
 1. Read number to be rooted
 2. Check for negative value
 3. Initialize estimate
 4. Divide number by estimate
 5. Form average of quotient and estimate
 6. Error = estimate - average
 7. Estimate = average
 8. If error too big, loop to 4
 9. Print number, estimate, error
10. Stop
```

After the prospective program's function has thus been adequately represented, the program can be written in practically any programming language. The above example of pseudocode could serve in the pursuit of an earlier exercise.

4.4 Top-Down Program Design

Flowcharts and pseudocode have the common feature of computer language independence. You do not have to be familiar with a programming language to comprehend a program's function. Moreover, a program represented in either form could be implemented in any of several computer languages. A further similarity is that each form allows the program function to be represented at successively finer levels of detail. One diagram can, for instance, represent only the gross features of a program. Other diagrams can represent details, and still other diagrams can detail the details to whatever degree necessary for adequate specification. Program planning, which begins with consideration of the gross features (program top) and proceeds to consider several levels of subsequent detail, is presently referred to as **top-down design** or **stagewise refinement** of the program. The accompanying series of flow diagrams illustrates this procedure.

For purposes of illustration, envision a program to monitor one month's activity in the checking account of one customer at the Primitive Bank and Trust. An initial meeting with PB&T's chief cashier has yielded agreement regarding the gross program functions. These are represented in the flowchart in Figure 2. At the beginning of each month, the customer's account balance is established and the counts of checks and deposits cleared to zero, etc. Each check written and each deposit constitute a transaction. The transactions and an end-of-month signal are the input to the program. At the end of the month, the program is to produce a summary of the transactions in the customer's account. The diagram in Figure 2 would certainly help communicate the gross program function, but most would agree it is inadequate for representing in Fortran code. A moment's consideration confirms the need for further details regarding "Set Initial Conditions" and "Process Transaction" before coding can optimally begin. With regard to the latter, we recognize the need to distinguish between a deposit and a check. This leads to a new (or, in terms of "top-down," a lower), more detailed level of representation. Such is presented in Figure 3a.

Figure 3a represents the "Process Transaction" rectangle from Figure 2, but in greater detail. The representation in Figure 3a shows a branching to one of two process blocks, after deciding whether the transaction is a check or a deposit. This is

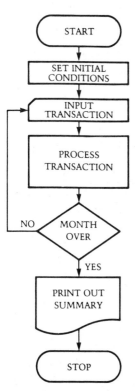

Figure 2. Top level flow diagram for Primitive Bank & Trust summary program

mildly reassuring, but the level represented is still too coarse to facilitate coding. Further detail is needed. For example, in processing a check a paramount consideration is whether the customer's account is overdrawn. This concern is reflected in Figure 3b. After reducing the customer's balance by the amount of the check, a test is to be made. If the account is overdrawn, the overdraft processing swings into action. This still lower level is represented in Figure 3c.

Further steps of refinement and similar steps taken with respect to other top-level elements yield low-level diagrams which can be specifically represented in program instructions. Each level is represented in the diagram by a block with one input and one output. Each low-level block is translated into a corresponding group or block of program instructions. The whole program is derived by figuratively stacking low-level blocks inside higher level blocks. The combination of sections of code developed in this way yields a program with identifiable structure. As should be evident from this example, the diagrams help us identify the details in the program function. Next, they help us prepare the program code and, if program malfunction subsequently rears its ugly head, help the responsible humans locate the cause of trouble.

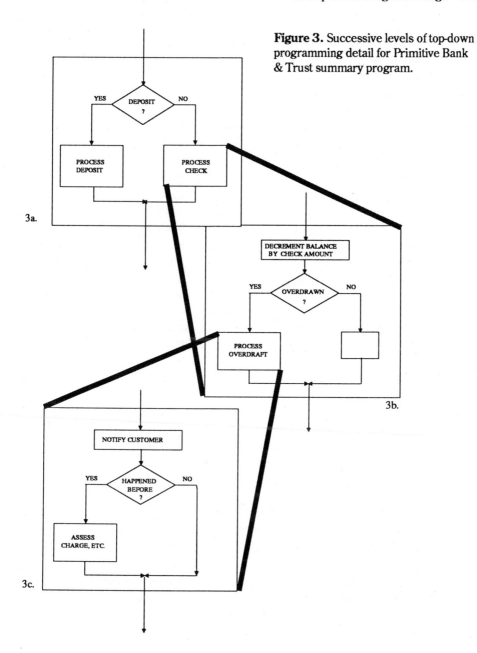

Figure 3. Successive levels of top-down programming detail for Primitive Bank & Trust summary program.

4.5 Program Documentation

The principal purpose of documentation is to record a program's purpose and origin and to provide auxiliary information which may be necessary or helpful for interpreting and using the program. When a substantial program is to be distributed widely and used in different circumstances, the need for documentation can become intense. Frequently the documentation is in the form of a manual which accompanies the program. In addition to information enabling contact with the program author and general explanation, this usually includes a sample data set and sample results. Other documentation can take the form of a tutorial sequence which introduces the program a step at a time. All this seems out of place when considering a typical beginner's program of a dozen lines of code, and frequently beginners become skilled in overlooking the need to document their efforts. Nonetheless, even the most trivial program deserves some documentation. The need usually can be met with suitable program comments. The examples presented in earlier sections usually have included minimum commenting, although to limit the length of the examples some desirable comments have been omitted, for example, the introduction of variables by name and purpose in comments at the beginning of a program.

Some programmers seem to get carried away with comments. They strive for certain ratios between the number of comments and the number of program instructions. Others insist on elaborate comment blocks at designated spots in each program. A milder approach holds that any arbitrary level of commenting may be excessive for some circumstances yet inadequate for others.

4.6 Summary

An optimum approach to the preparation of any computer program necessarily involves some planning. The degree to which the planning is done will be different for different programmers and different situations. Simple situations may require little more than a specification of the information to be processed and the form and substance of the output. For more involved projects, the gross purpose will be reduced to components and these in turn to components of components, to arrive at a specification of the actual steps to be represented in program code. In most instances, the preparation of code will proceed only after an adequate specification is in hand. With such a specification in hand, those who program only infrequently may find the guide that follows to be of service.

References

1. Davis, Gordon B., and Hoffman, Thomas R. *Fortran 77: A Structured, Disciplined Style.* New York: McGraw-Hill, 1983.

2. Diday, Rich and Page, Rex. *Fortran for Humans.* St. Paul, MN: West, 1981.

3. Leimkuhl, Nonna Kliss. *Fortran 77, A Top-Down Approach.* New York: Macmillan, 1983.

4. Merchant, Michael J. *Fortran 77, Language and Style.* Belmont, CA: Wadsworth, 1981.

5. Spencer, Donald B. *Problems for Computer Solution.* Ormond Beach, FL: Camelot, 1977.

6. Tropp, H.S., and Lee, J. A. N. (Editors). Fortran's Twenty-Fifth Anniversary. *Annals of the History of Computing*, vol. 6, no. 1, January, 1984.

Quick Guide to Frequently-Used Fortran Forms

Fortran form	Topic	See page
Declaration (must precede all executable instructions)		
REAL ABM,IPO	Establishes ABM and IPO as REAL variables. If declaration were omitted, IPO would be INTEGER.	44
INTEGER MN, PLO	Establishes MN and PLO as INTEGER variables. If declaration were omitted, PLO would be REAL.	44
CHARACTER*5 CX	Establishes CX as a CHARACTER variable, capable of holding 5 characters. If *5 omitted, CX would hold only one character.	46
DIMENSION B2(20)	Establishes B2 as a 20-element array; default type is REAL.	50
REAL MX(-10:20)	Establishes MX as a 31-element, REAL array; subscript for the first element is -10.	54
INTEGER ZP(10,5)	Establishes ZP as an INTEGER array with 10 rows and 5 columns.	84
CHARACTER*3 PX(50,80)	Establishes PX as a 50 by 80 CHARACTER array, each array element can hold 3 characters.	46,87
Assignment		
ARD = 12.5	Assignment of real constant to real variable; declaration of variable optional.	7
JKL = 77	Assignment of integer constant to integer variable; declaration optional.	17
CHA = 'LL'	Assignment of character constant to character variable; declaration mandatory.	46
DATA X,Y,M/2*3.0,5/	DATA statement assigns 3.0 to real variables X and Y, and 5 to integer variable M.	77
Order of Operations		
( )	Operations within parentheses done first.	9
AB ** CD ** EF	Exponentiation done next, from right to left.	10
XX * YY / ZZ	Multiplications and divisions done next, from left to right.	10
PP + DD - QQ	Additions and subtractions done last.	10

Quick Guide to Frequently-Used Fortran Forms *(continued)*

Fortran form	Topic	See page
Output		
PRINT*, A,B,J,K	Free-format print, standard output fields.	10
PRINT 101, X 101 FORMAT(1X,F8.3)	Formatted output of real; value appears in an 8-column field, 3 columns to right of d.p.	65
PRINT 102, M 102 FORMAT(1X,I7)	Formatted output of integer; value appears right-justified in 7-column field.	73
PRINT 103, CH 103 FORMAT(1X,A6)	Formatted output of character; output left-justified in 6-column field.	73
WRITE(*,*) X,Y,M	Free-format write to standard output with standard width fields.	11
WRITE(*,105) L,M 105 FORMAT(1X,I10,I4)	Formatted write of two integers to standard output with different fields.	73
WRITE(3,*) B,C	Free-format write to non-standard output. Unit 3 must be opened, file named.	116
WRITE(4,108) K,A 108 FORMAT(1X,I3,F8.2)	Formatted write to non-standard output. Unit 4 must be opened, file named.	117
Open/Close		
OPEN(UNIT=3,FILE='ROSTER',STATUS='OLD') OPEN(UNIT=4,FILE='LISTER',STATUS='NEW') . . . CLOSE(UNIT=3) CLOSE(UNIT=4) .	Opens files for access and creation by program.	113
Looping		
DO 10 K = 1,6 . 6 CONTINUE	Plain DO loop; all operations between DO and CONTINUE repeated 6 times.	18
. READ*,(B(L),L=1,20)	Implied DO loop for reading into array B; the array must be declared with dimension at least 20.	57

DO 8 M = 1,9,2
  DO 4 N = 1,10
  .
  .
4   CONTINUE
8 CONTINUE
	Nested DO loops. Outer loop executed 5 times as control variable M takes on values 1,3,5,7 and 9. Inner, DO 4 loop executes 10 times for each iteration of the outer, DO 8 loop.	55

Quick Guide to Frequently-Used Fortran Forms *(continued)*

Fortran form	Topic	See page
Looping (continued)		

`REAL DC(5,20)`
 	
`DO 22 IR=1,5`
`    PRINT 18,(DC(IR,IC),IC=1,20)`
`22 CONTINUE`
`18 FORMAT(1X,20F4.1)`
	Implied DO nested within a regular DO. During each of five iterations of the regular DO 22 loop, the implied DO prints out 20 values.	88

Conditional Execution

Fortran form	Topic	See page
`IF(condition)A=3.0` `    (next)`	Standard logical IF. If condition is true, 3.0 is assigned to variable A, then control transfers to (next). If condition tests false, A is unchanged, control transfers to (next). Note: no ENDIF.	25

`IF(condition)THEN`
`.`
`.`
`ENDIF`
	Block IF. If condition is true, all instructions in the block are executed, if not true, all are skipped. ENDIF essential.	30

`IF(condition)THEN`
`    (then    block)`
`ELSE`
`    (else    block)`
`ENDIF`
	IF-THEN-ELSE blocks. If condition is true, the THEN block is executed, the ELSE block skipped. If condition is not true, the THEN block is skipped and the ELSE block executed. Note ENDIF.	32

`IF(cond1)THEN`
`.`
`    IF(cond2)THEN`
`.`
`    ENDIF`
`.`
`ENDIF`
	Nested block IF's. Each IF has its own ENDIF and each ENDIF refers to most recently preceding IF.	106

`IF(cond1)THEN`
`.`
`    ELSEIF(cond2)THEN`
`.`
`    ELSE`
`.`
`ENDIF`
	Three-block IF with ELSEIF. Only one block will be executed; only one ENDIF needed.	107

`DO 20 IR=1,100`
`    IF(cond)THEN`
`.`
`    ENDIF`
`.`
`20 CONTINUE`
	IF block inside DO loop. The block must be completed within the loop.	47

`IF(cond)THEN`
`    DO 10 I=1,10`
`.`
`10    CONTINUE`
`ENDIF`
	DO loop inside block IF. The loop must complete inside IF block.	32

Quick Guide to Frequently-Used Fortran Forms *(continued)*

Fortran form	Topic	See page
Input		
`READ*, A,B,M`	Free-format read searches along data row for values to fill variables in read list. Blank spaces separate data values, include decimal points with real data but NOT with integer data. Character data must be enclosed in single quotes.	27

`DO 10 IR=1,40`
`   READ*, X,Y,Z`
`       .`
`10 CONTINUE`
	Free-format read within regular DO loop. At least one new data row will be accessed each time control transfers to the READ.	28

`    READ 101, AB,MN` `101 FORMAT(3X,F6.1,I8)`	Formatted read of real and integer values from one data row. The first three columns are skipped by the 3X.	77
`    READ 102, AB,CD` `102 FORMAT(2F10.4)`	Formatted read of data values into real variables. If decimal point included in datum, the included d.p. overrides the FORMAT. If no d.p. included, one will be provided by the FORMAT.	75
`    READ 103, IK,MM` `103 FORMAT(2I8)`	Formatted read of data values into integer variables. Data values must be right-justified in the 8-column fields.	73

`    CHARACTER*3 BB`
`    READ 104, BB`
`104 FORMAT(2X,A3)`
	Formatted read into 3-character variable using alphanumeric field specification. If character capacity of variable and column count don't match, values are left-justified.	73

`READ(*,*) D,N`	Alternative free-format read from standard input.	27
`    READ(3,107) A,K` `107 FORMAT(F10.2,I4)`	Formatted read from non-standard input. Unit 3 must be opened, file named.	115

Quick Guide to Frequently-Used Fortran Forms *(continued)*

Fortran form	Topic	See page
Subprograms		

```
C MAIN PROGRAM
      .
      .
      ZP=BX(X,Y,M)
   ┌─► .
   │    \\\
   │     \\\
   │      \\\
   │       \\\
   │  END   \\\
   │         \\\
   │          \\\
   │           \\\
   │  FUNCTION BX(A,B,K)
   │    .
   │    .
   │  BX= . . .
   │    .
   └─ RETURN
      END
```

The principal Fortran subprograms are the FUNCTION and the SUBROUTINE; either can include any number of statements and can accomodate input and output.

Subprogram calls can originate in the main program or in another subprogram. Call a FUNCTION by including the subprogram name in the operation part of a Fortran instruction. In the main program here, BX has not been declared as an array, so it will be recognized as the name of a FUNCTION.

Values transfer from main to subprogram based on corresponding position; the value given X in main is available in subprogram as the value of A, etc. Variables in subprogram list must agree with those in call both in data type and in number.

Function subprogram established by FUNCTION followed by subprogram name and list of variables used. Subprogram name must appear alone on left of equals at least once. The name and the variables serve to return values to main. Control returns from FUNCTION to the point it was called. One END and at least one RETURN are essential.

92,95

| *Subroutines* | | |

```
C MAIN PROGRAM
      REAL AC(10)
      .
      .
      CALL ZAP(AC,P,D,J)
   ┌─► .
   │    \\\
   │     \\\
   │  END  \\\
   │  SUBROUTINE ZAP(R,S,T,N)
   │  REAL R(10)
   │    .
   │    .
   │  S= . . .
   │  T= . . .
   │    .
   └─ RETURN
      .
      END
```

Invoke a subroutine with a CALL instruction followed by subroutine name and argument list. Values transfer based on position; P's value in main is S's value in ZAP, etc.

Argument lists must agree in data type and number.

Subroutine established by SUBROUTINE followed by subprogram name and variable list. If argument list includes an array, it must be declared the same way in main and in the subprogram. Subroutine name must not be used, values transferred via variable lists.

Control returns to main statement next after the CALL.

95

Index

A (alphanumeric) FORMAT, 73
ABS, ACOS, ALOG, ALOG10, ASIN,
ATAN (library functions), 34
Accumulating a sum, 20
Adjustable subprogram arrays, 98
AIMAG, 111
.AND., 105
Apostrophe (single quote mark)
in CHARACTER data, 47, 78
in free FORMAT, 21
in FORMAT, 70
Argument, 33, 92
Arithmetic operations, 9, 10
Arithmetic statement function, 91
Array (subscripted variable), 50, 83
as argument in CALL, 97
dimension, 50
element, 51
initializing, 56, 59
input/output, 57, 59
Assignment operator (equals sign), 7
Asterisk, 9, 78
Auxiliary storage, 112

Bar graph example, 56
Blank COMMON, 101
Blanks, 28
Block IF, 30
BN, BZ, 77
Break (reset), 4

CALL, 95
Calling, 33, 92
Carriage control (line printer), 71
Catalog (directory), 5
CHAR, 48
CHARACTER, 46
constants, 46
functions, 48
strings, substrings, 47
variables, 46
Checking output, 38

Clearing array, 56, 59, 62, 87
CLOSE statement, 115, 133
CMPLX, 111
Collating sequence, 48
Column, 5, 7
index, 5, 88
Comments in program, 19
COMMON, 101, 103
Compiler, compiling, 2
COMPLEX, 110
Compound LOGICAL (multiple
consideration structure), 105
Computing something, 6
Computed GO TO, 120
Concatenation, 48
Conditional execution, 25, 63, 134
Conditional transfer of control, 25
Constants, 8
CHARACTER, 46
COMPLEX, 110
DOUBLE PRECISION, 109
INTEGER (fixed point), 15
LOGICAL, 104
REAL (floating point), 15, 44
Continuation, 22, 35, 52, 70, 102
CONTINUE, 18
Control (CTRL) key, 4
Control of looping
by condition, 63
by counter, 18
Control of program in system, 3
Control variable, 19
Conversion of type, 45
COS, 34

D FORMAT specification, 109
DABS, DCOS, DSIN, etc., 110
DATA, data, 77
Data type (mode), 15
Debugging (program troubles), 36
Declaring data type, 44, 132
Default data type, 44
Diagnostic (error) messages, 37
DIMENSION, 50
Direct access files, 113
Directory (file catalog), 5

Disk (magnetic storage), 113
Division, 10
Division symbol, used to skip an output line, 70
DO, 18
   implied, 57
   nested, 55
Documentation, 130
Double-alternative decision structure, 32
DOUBLE PRECISION, 109
Dummy variables (parameters), 92

E FORMAT specification, 68
Echo print, 29, 39
Editor, editing, 5
Element (statement of instruction), 7
ELSEIF, 106
Embedded blanks (BZ, BN), 77
END (of program), 11
END= (detect end of data file), 76, 116
ENDIF, 31
Endless loop, 39
ENDWHILE, 63
Equals sign (assignment operator), 7
EQUIVALENCE, 121
ERR= (detect input error), 76
Error messages, 36, 37
Escape, 4
Exercises, 13, 22, 39, 49, 62, 71, 78, 89, 96, 118
EXP, 34
Exponential form, 68
Exponentiation, 10, 17
Expression (operation), 7
EXTERNAL, 100
External, 93
   storage, 112

Factorial, 14, 22
.FALSE., 104
Fibonacci number exercise, 62
Field, 10
Field specification (format types),
   A, 73
   D, 109
   E, 68

Field specification, *continued*
   F, 67
   I, 73
   L, 105
   X, 67
File directory (catalog), 5
Files, 5, 11
   direct access, 112
   sequential, 116
Fixed point (INTEGER type), 27
FLOAT (REAL), 45
Floating point (REAL type), 27
Flowcharts, 125, 127
FORMAT statement, 10, 65, 73
Fortran, 2
Fortran compiler, 2
Fractions in integer arithemetic, 17
Free FORMAT (list-directed I/O), 10
Function, 33
   arithmetic statement, 91
   CHARACTER, 48
   INTEGER, 45
   library (supplied, intrinsic), 33
   subprogram, 92

.GE., .GT., 26
GO TO (GOTO), 64, 126
   computed, 120
Graphic output, 56, 87
Guide to Fortran Forms, 132

Heirarchy (order) of operations
   arithmetic, 10
   logical, 106

I field specification, 73
IABS, 34
ICHAR, 49
IF, 25
   block, 30
IFIX, 45
IF-THEN, 31
IF-THEN-ELSE, 32
Implicit typing, 118
Implied DO, 57
Implied mode (type), 8, 42
Incrementing loop index, 58
Initializing, 19, 36

Input (see also I/O), 135
Instruction (statement), 7
INT, 34, 45

INTEGER, 16, 27
  arithmetic, 17
  constants, 15
  declaration, 44
  exponentiation, 17
  variables, 17
INTRINSIC, 100
Instrinsic (library) functions, 33
I/O (input/output), 10, 27, 65, 73

Job control, 12
Justify, 73

L FORMAT specification, 105
.LE., .LT., 26
Labeled COMMON, 103
Labeling output
  with free FORMAT, 21
  with FORMAT, 70
Library functions, 33
Line printer, 10, 71
List, 11, 28
List-directed output, 27
  output, 10
Literal output (labels), 21, 70
LOGICAL, 104
Logical declaration, 104
Logical (standard) IF, 25
Logical operators, 105
  heirarchy, 106
Loop increment, 58
Loop index, 19, 21
Loops and looping, 18, 55, 63, 119, 133
  DO, 18
  implied DO, 57
  nested DO, 55
  WHILE-DO, 63

Machine language, 2
Magnetic disk, 112
Main program, 91
Maxint, 24
MAX0, MIN0, 45
Memory, 112

Mixed type (mode) operation, 16, 44
Mnemonic variable names, 21
MOD, 34
Mode (type), 15, 44
Multiple alternative, 106
Multiple consideration, 107
Multiple subscripts, 107
Multiplication, 9

Names for files, 5
.NE., 26
.NOT., 105
Nested loops, 55
Newline (return) key, 4
NINT, 34, 35
Normal exit from loop, 19

Objectives (three levels), 2, 43, 82
OPEN, 113, 133
Operating system, 3
Operation (expression), 7
Operation symbols
  arithmetic, 8, 10
  logical, 105
  relational, 26
.OR., 105
Ordering operations, 9, 132
Output (see also I/O), 133
  list-directed (free FORMAT), 10
  with FORMAT control, 65
Overflow of output field, 68

P (scale factor), 69
Page skip (printer control), 71
PARAMETER declaration, 119
Parameter (dummy variable), 92
Parens (parentheses), 9
Physical record, 113
PRINT statement, 66
PRINT* statement, 21
Program, 2
Program planning, 124
Program troubles, 36
Programmed file management, 111
Pseudocode, 126

Radians, 34, 36
READ statement, 65

READ* statement, 28
REAL, 34
    constants, 15
    declaration, 44
    statement, 45
    variables, 15
Record, 112
Relational operators, 26
Repeated fields, 67, 69
Reset, 4
RETURN, 93
Return (new line) key, 4
Returned, 33
REWIND, 117, 118
Row, 5

Scale factor, 70
Scientific notation, 68
Search for max or min, 61
Sentinel (end of data), 88
Sequential files, 112, 116
Shift key, 4
SIN, SINH, 34
Slash (division symbol) in FORMAT, 70
Sorting example, 58
Specification (declaration) statement,
    44
SQRT, 33, 34
Stagewise refinement, 127
Standard input/output (I/O), 112
Statement (instruction), 7
Statement function, 91

Statement number (label), 19, 38
STOP, 26
String (character), 46
Subprograms, 90, 136
Subroutines, 95, 136
Subscripted variables (arrays), 50, 83
Substring (character), 47
Summaries, 42, 81, 122, 130
Supplied (library) functions, 34
Symbols for flowchart, 128

TAN, 34
.TRUE., 104
Terminals, 3
THEN, 31
Top-down program development, 127
Transfer of control, 18, 25, 33, 64
Truncation, 17
TYPE (mode) of data, 15, 44
    conversion, 45
    specification, 44

Unconditional transfer (GO TO), 64
Underflow, 68
Unformatted record, 113
User subprograms, 90

Variables, 8
    subscripted, 50, 83

WHILE-DO, 63
WRITE statement, 11, 114

X field specification, 67